Conflict Management For

CAMPUS PUBLIC SAFETY

Non-Escalation, De-Escalation, and Crisis Intervention For Law Enforcement and Security Professionals

Gary T. Klugiewicz

Dave Young

Allen Oelschlaeger

For bulk-purchasing pricing, please contact:

Vistelar
1845 N. Farwell Ave., Suite 210
Milwaukee, WI 53202
Phone: 877-690-8230
Fax: 866-406-2374
Email: info@vistelar.com
Web: www.vistelar.com

Authors: Gary T. Klugiewicz, Dave Young and Allen Oelschlaeger
Contributor: Lt. Jill Weisensel, M.S.

Conflict Management For Campus Public Safety

ISBN-13: 978-0-9976791-9-9
ISBN-10: 0-9976791-9-0

BISAC Subject Headings:
LAW / Ethics & Professional Responsibility
LAW / Criminal Law / General
PSYCHOLOGY / Education & Training

Published By Truths Publishing, Milwaukee, WI
Printed In the United States of America

Table of Contents

Table of Contents *continued*

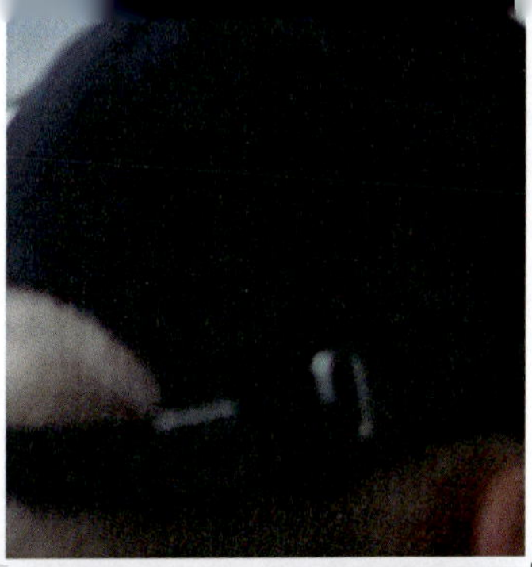

Introduction

About This Manual

This manual was developed as a resource for campus public safety professionals and was developed in partnership with the International Association of Campus Law Enforcement Administrators.

However, the principles of customer service and conflict management covered in this manual also have value to anyone within a campus environment who would benefit from knowing how to better manage conflict with students, among campus staff, between supervisors and employees and between campus departments.

This is the course manual for Vistelar's *Conflict Management* in-person and online training programs for campus public safety professionals and is a great companion to any of Vistelar's *Confidence in Conflict* books. It can also be used as a stand-alone guide for learning how to verbally de-escalate situations (therefore reducing the number of use-of-force incidents) and better manage conflict.

In the first part of this manual, you will learn Vistelar's core principle of conflict management, how to behave in alignment with this principle, and how to identify and develop "guards" against triggers to conflict. Also explained are Vistelar's 6 Cs of Conflict Management: *Point-Of-Impact Conflict Management Framework*™ — and its *Systemized Structure of Tactics* that make Vistelar's methodologies easy to learn, remember, apply and teach. The remainder of this manual focuses on the "how-tos" of each of these tactics, including a key component of de-escalation known as proxemic management.

At the end of this manual, everything you have learned is summarized.

Whether you are reading this manual as a component of a live class or online program, in conjunction with one of our books, or in isolation from any other Vistelar training offering, we look forward to you becoming a master at conflict management.

Benefits

After reading this manual — especially if read in conjunction with another Vistelar training opportunity (e.g., live training) — you will be better prepared to respond professionally to conflict and effectively manage conflict it in both your professional and personal lives. However, our primary goal is officer safety.

You will gain the *knowledge*, *skills* and *abilities* to interact with anyone — in person, by phone or in writing — and to:

- Engage in a way to not cause conflict or unnecessarily escalate situations
- Confidently and professionally deal with questioning, anger, and verbal abuse
- Participate in difficult conversations and mediate positive outcomes

GOAL

WORK ENVIRONMENT AND PERSONAL RELATIONSHIPS INCOMPATIBLE WITH VIOLENCE

- Effectively de-escalate conflict and remain safe in crisis situations
- Persuade others to cooperate
- Know what to do and how to do it when resistance or aggression results in physical engagement
- End an interaction in a better place than where it started
- Look good on camera no matter where an interaction ends up
- If necessary, articulate a defense for taking appropriate action

The outcomes of this training will bring benefits to students, campus staff, your campus public safety agency, and yourself.

The results within your agency include:

- Higher levels of student and campus staff satisfaction[1]
- Improved team performance, morale and safety[2]
- Reduced complaints, liabilities and injuries[3]
- Protected reputation, culture and agency continuity[4]
- Reduced harm from emotional or physical violence[5]
- Decreased stress levels, lateral violence and bullying[6]
- Less compassion fatigue, absenteeism and turnover
- Not having a damaging video show up on YouTube or the evening news

Who Is Vistelar

Vistelar's training focuses on addressing the entire spectrum of human conflict at the point of impact — from before an interaction begins through to the consequences of how an interaction is managed.

We offer a wide range of training programs that address how to:

- Provide better customer service
- Predict, prevent and mitigate conflict
- Avert verbal and physical attacks
- De-escalate conflict
- Control crisis and aggression
- Handle physical violence

All of our training programs address the reality that, at the point of impact with a person of authority, most people ask themselves these "Four Great American Questions:" 1) Who are you? 2) Where do you get your authority? 3) Why are you here? 4) What's in it for me? – which includes these four benefits (P.O.L.E.)

- Physical Safety: improved threat assessment and physical assault avoidance
- Organizational Safety: better job performance, morale and collaboration
- Legal Safety: less risk of personal liability and looking bad on YouTube
- Emotional Safety: improved relationships, self-confidence and life quality

TRAINING PROGRAMS

ENTIRE SPECTRUM OF HUMAN CONFLICT

NON-ESCALATION DE-ESCALATION

Conflict Management For:
- Gatekeeper Staff
- Contact Professionals
- Crisis First Responders

PHYSICAL ALTERNATIVES

- Principles of Subject Control 1 & 2
- Non-Lethal Weapons
- Lethal Weapons

Over 50 Specialty Courses

Tactics taught, relative emphasis on each tactic, and level of intrusiveness depend on student's rules of engagement, environments, applications and roles within their organization

Speaking - Workshops - Instructor Schools
Live - Online - Blended

VISTELAR *Addressing The Entire Spectrum Of Human Conflict*

Our training is focused on the point of impact — the short period of time when disagreements, insults or gateway behaviors, like swearing or aggressive posturing, can escalate to conflict and on to emotional and/or physical violence, with the goal of:

- Looking good on camera
- Choreographing your response
- Communicating concern

Vistelar's training supports the best practice recommendations outlined in the International Association of Chiefs of Police (IACP) *National Consensus Policy on Use of Force*, as well as supports these three principles from the *Final Report of the President's Task Force on 21st Century Policing*.

- Embrace a Guardian, versus Warrior, Mindset
- Adopt Procedural Justice (emphasis on how people are treated rather than just fairness of the outcome)
- Encourage Community Engagement (support of trust-building/non-enforcement activities)

Who Is Vistelar *continued*

Vistelar's methodologies have been proven in real-world environments for over thirty years and are the subject of several books and training manuals in Vistelar's *Confidence In Conflict* series.

We offer our training via speaking engagements, workshops, and instructor schools using both live and online methods of instruction.

Our vision is to make the world safer by teaching everyone how to treat each other with dignity by showing respect.

POINT-OF-IMPACT CONFLICT MANAGEMENT TRAINING

LEARN HOW TO:

- Provide better customer service
- Predict, prevent and mitigate conflict
- Avert verbal and physical attacks
- De-escalate conflict
- Control crisis and aggression
- Handle physical violence

BENEFITS:

- Higher levels of customer satisfaction
- Reduced complaints, liabilities & injuries
- Improved team performance and morale
- Protected reputation, culture, business continuity and employee safety
- Reduced workplace violence
- Not having a damaging video show up on YouTube or the evening news

WHO WE TRAIN:

- Contact professionals who directly interact with the general public or an organization's clients
- Organizational teams who want to improve their performance by better managing conflict.

Foundations

Conflict Primer

Do you experience conflict in your personal life and at your work within campus public safety? Sure you do, all officers do.

While not immediately obvious, well-managed conflict can actually result in positive outcomes. It leads to identification of problems, innovation to solve those problems and development of new skills. Without conflict, progress would come to a standstill.

Consider an officer attending a campus meeting. Without conflict, no ideas to address the issues would be brought up and campus problems would continue.

However, it is when conflict is poorly managed that challenges occur. Mismanaged conflict with students and the general public can result in complaints, liabilities and injuries. Within a campus public safety agency, it can diminish performance, morale and safety. Further, innovation stops, collaboration is stymied, turnover skyrockets and productivity drops. Within a family, it can ruin relationships and at its worse it can result in mental health issues and suicide. And finally, if caught on camera and posted to YouTube or the evening news, poorly managed conflict can destroy reputations.

In some instances, poorly-managed conflict within organizations can even escalate to workplace violence in the form of both verbal and physical assault. Such violence can originate from customers, co-workers, personal relations, or someone with criminal intent. Workplace violence can exact a heavy emotional and physical toll on those involved, both immediately and over the long term.

In addition, poorly-managed conflict by a campus public safety professional can obviously escalate to violence in the form of both verbal and physical assault.

"Peace is not absence of conflict, it is the ability to handle conflict by peaceful means."
Ronald Reagan, President of the United States (1911-2004)

One reason conflict is so prevalent is because, beyond criminal activity, it arises from disagreements, insults and gateway behaviors, like swearing or aggressive posturing, which frequently just rolls off people's backs. However, for a wide variety of reasons, things sometimes escalate.

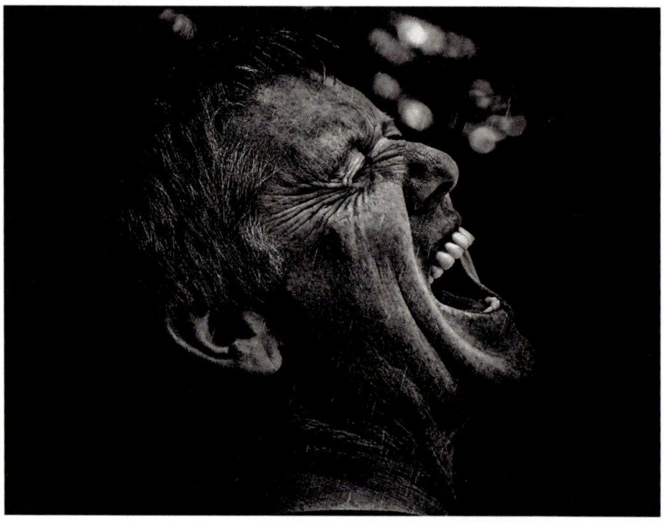

In this program you will learn how to predict and prevent this escalation, and if necessary, de-escalate a situation by effectively managing the conflict. You will also learn how to end an interaction to achieve the best possible outcome and establish a strong foundation for the next interaction. Finally, if you struggle at all with conflict, you will gain confidence to deal with it head-on, rather than avoiding it or accommodating people by giving in just to appease them.

In summary, conflict is inevitable in campus public safety; you cannot eliminate it. However, if well managed, it drives student, faculty, and staff satisfaction, team performance, problem solving, innovation, collaboration and, most importantly, officer safety. If conflict is poorly managed, it can create a myriad of problems including emotional and physical injuries.

OUTCOMES OF POORLY MANAGED CONFLICT

WITHIN AN ORGANIZATION:
COMPLAINTS, LIABILITIES, AND INJURIES

WITHIN A TEAM:
DIMINISHED PERFORMANCE, MORALE, AND SAFETY

IF CAUGHT ON CAMERA:
DESTROYED REPUTATIONS

Core Principle

Let us start with the core principle of customer service and conflict management that serves as the foundation for everything we teach.

Surprisingly, many organizations are just now discovering the importance of this principle. For example, between 2013 and 2015, Google researched the role of conflict in team effectiveness. They conducted scores of interviews, observed hundreds of teams and analyzed tens of thousands of pieces of data. But, for a long time, they were stuck. Charles Duhigg, in his book Smarter, Faster, Better, quotes a person who worked on this project:

> *"We knew it was important for people to feel like they can speak up if something's wrong. But those are also the behaviors that can set people at odds. We didn't know why some groups could clash and still perform, while others would hit a period of conflict and everything would fall apart."*

After two years of work, the Google researchers concluded that all the team factors they thought would make a difference did not seem to matter at all. They could not find any correlation between team effectiveness and such factors as who was on the team, co-location of team members and use of consensus decision-making.

What they found was just one team attribute that made all the difference in team effectiveness. Teams with it performed exceptionally, and teams without it struggled.

Not surprisingly, this one attribute is identical to Vistelar's core principle of customer service and conflict management.

CORE PRINCIPLE OF CONFLICT MANAGEMENT

TREAT PEOPLE WITH DIGNITY BY SHOWING RESPECT, EVEN IF YOU DISAGREE WITH THEM

Treat people with dignity by showing respect even if you disagree with them.

We all know acknowledging people's inherent value as human beings is the right thing to do, but we also know individuals sometimes make mistakes in how they treat other people.

Dignity: our inherent value as human beings
This stands in contrast to respect, which is earned through one's actions

Why is it that we do not value dignity and always treat each other as fellow human beings? There are three reasons:

1. People do not understand that treating people with dignity, regardless of the circumstances, drives better results and is a self-serving act. Within campus public safety, if you treat everyone as human beings, you will have better relationships, improved job performance, increased work satisfaction and better field outcomes. If you treat people with dignity, they will more likely cooperate with requests, not get upset and treat you well in return.

> *"When differences divide us, treating each other with dignity by showing respect establishes the common ground for managing conflict."*
>
> from Vistelar's *Treat People Right* card

2. Treating people with dignity is not a natural response, especially when you disagree with them or they are treating you poorly. This type of response requires training to overcome and most people do not receive such training.

3. People do not know the well-proven specific tactics for treating people with dignity.

Please Note ...

"The Google experience points to the face that conflict is inevitable in all professions. What's different between professions are the established rules of engagement. Within law enforcement, treating people with dignity is good for results and good for the officer but, like Google discovered, it is hard to teach. Law enforcement officers deal with many situations where people are at their worst. Over time, just to keep sane, officers become desensitized, which creates a 'he/she doesn't deserve to be treated well' mentality. We need to constantly remind ourselves that treating people with dignity is good for results and good for the officer."

Kevin Shults, Major, Broward County Sheriff's Office, Florida

In this manual, you will continue to be reminded of the importance of treating people with dignity to drive better results and you will be taught how to overcome your natural reactions to disagreements and being treated poorly. More importantly, you will learn the specific tactics for how to treat people with dignity, especially difficult people. That is the primary focus of this program.

The first thing to know about how to treat people with dignity is that, in order to do so, you must show them respect.

This does not mean that you need to respect everyone. That would be impossible since respect is based on your personal values and must be earned. However, it is essential that you show everyone respect. All people deserve to be shown respect.

How To Show Respect

Diversity education teaches the proper way to treat people of different backgrounds, races and genders. This can be challenging given the subtleties of cross-cultural expectations.

To be effective at customer service and conflict management, you must realize how ALL people want to be treated, regardless of their race, religion, gender, sexual orientation, culture, etc.

All people want to be shown respect and here are the five approaches for doing this:

1. See world through their eyes
2. Listen with all senses
3. Ask and explain why
4. Offer options, let them choose
5. Give opportunity to reconsider

These five approaches describe how all people want to be treated. Everyone wants to be shown empathy, listened to, asked to do something rather than being told, provided an explanation for why they are being asked, offered options to choose from, and given an opportunity to rethink a decision.

Here is a further explanation of each of the five approaches to showing people respect.

1. See World Through Their Eyes

Showing empathy, which is taking another person's perspective, enables you to treat that person the way you would want to be treated if you were him or her and in the exact same circumstances. Doing this with everyone produces better outcomes.

Example: "You must be worried about your friend," and then pause and truly listen to what he or she might have to say.

2. Listen With All Senses

The most powerful way to show respect to human beings is to listen to them, which is a much different practice than just hearing them. You hear raindrops, but to truly listen to people you must use all your senses. Besides just hearing the other person's words and tone of voice, be attentive to visual cues like facial expression, eye contact, posture and body language — as well as smell (been drinking?), touch (tense?) and taste (smoker?) cues.

Example: Listen to a student's concerns about your agency, rather than just hearing his or her words while you're trying to formulate a response in your head.

3. Ask and Explain Why

How To Show People Respect

- See world through their eyes
- Listen with all senses
- Ask and explain why
- Offer options, let them choose
- Give opportunity to reconsider

Every time you would like someone to do something, make a conscious effort to ask him or her to do it rather than tell them. Show people respect by asking a question rather than barking a command. Asking is for human beings, telling is for dogs (sit, roll over, bark).

Then, once you have asked, make the assumption that people can be easily confused. Presume the individuals with whom you interact may not understand what is going on or have any idea what will happen next. Take the time to provide an explanation for why things are done as they are.

Realize that, if you don't explain why, the other person will likely fill in the blanks with their own reasons which could be incorrect and will probably be negative.

Ask Example: "Can you please come with me?" rather than the command "Come with me!"

Explain Why Example: "The reason I stopped you is because I recorded you driving eighty miles per hour when the posted speed limit is sixty."

4. Offer Options, Let Them Choose

People want to feel empowered to make their own decisions even when there are tight restrictions on their behavior. Look for ways to give people a couple of options from which to choose, rather than a single choice you have selected for them.

Example: "Would you rather call your roommate right now to come and get you or do you want to get an Uber or Lyft?"

5. Give Opportunity To Reconsider

People sometimes make mistakes. In the heat of the moment, they might make a rude comment or refuse a request. If there is no safety concern, allow them to save face and give them another chance.

Example: "Is there anything I can say to help you change your mind. I would hope so."

You may already be applying these five approaches for showing people respect in many of your interactions. However, remember the goal: to show respect to EVERYONE with whom you interact, ALL THE TIME.

Why? Because at the end of the day, doing so drives better results and is a self-serving act.

Practicing Empathy

Empathy is taking another person's perspective. It is the engine that drives the effectiveness of all Vistelar conflict management and non-escalation tactics.

"Empathy is about standing in someone else's shoes, feeling with his or her heart, seeing with his or her eyes."

Daniel H. Pink — best-selling author (1964 - present)

Empathy should not be confused with sympathy, which is a feeling of sorrow for another person's misfortune. To be effective at customer service and conflict management, there is no need or advantage to share in the sorrow and distress of others. Why? Because it can:

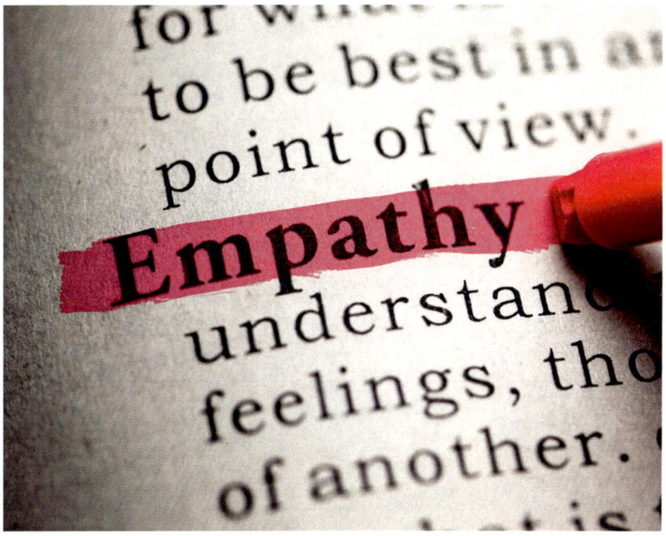

- Distract you from the task at hand
- Cloud your judgment in dealing with the conflict
- Affect your personal life

How do you practice *Empathy* with another person? By applying the *Empathy Triad*:

1. Acknowledge the other person's perspective. This first element of the *Empathy Triad* can be used when interacting with someone for the first time. In such situations, you know little about the other person so taking his or her perspective is difficult.

   Whatever the other person might say, you can respond with statements like: "Thank you for sharing that with me." — "Hmm, I never thought of it that way." — "Huh, that's interesting."

2. Seek to understand the other person. Try to understand his or her perspective so you can treat the individual the way you would want to be treated if you were that person and in the exact same circumstances.

   By listening to another person with all your senses, you can learn his or her needs, wants and desires (active intelligence gathering) and then, based on this newfound knowledge, treat the person the way you think he or she wants to be treated.

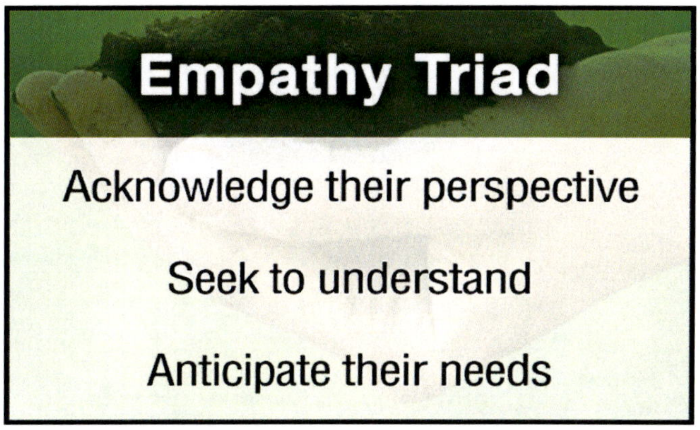

3. Anticipate the other person's needs. Consider what that person will be thinking or feeling immediately following

the interaction, the next day or later. The goal is to treat the other person the way that person may not even know he or she wants to be treated.

Having the capacity to practice this third element of the *Empathy Triad* is the "secret sauce" of customer service and conflict management and non-escalation.

Empathy is NOT sympathy. Nor is it agreeing with or respecting the thoughts or actions of another person.

Instead, *Empathy* is a professional approach for communicating concern and active intelligence gathering about where the other person is coming from. These are both essential components for providing excellent customer service and effectively managing a conflict situation.

Empathy Can Be Uncomfortable

Practicing empathy can be uncomfortable. For example, the response to a mother abusing her own child would be condemnation of the mother by almost everyone. However, that is not practicing empathy. An empathetic response would be to try to put yourself in the mother's shoes; to try to see the world through the mother's eyes. For most people, that would be uncomfortable, even painful, so they do not try. However, practicing empathy is a learned skill, at which you can only improve by trying. So, view that uncomfortable feeling as a challenge. Push through it and you will improve your ability to perform this valuable skill.

Empathy is often described as the golden rule: "Do unto others as you would have them do unto you." However, that is not an accurate description because it suggests treating others based on your perspective, rather than their perspective.

A better description of *Empathy* is: "Do unto others as you would have them do unto you, if you were them and were in the exact same circumstances."

That is *Empathy* — seeing the world through the other person's eyes instead of yours; understanding the other person's perspective.

Again, *Empathy* is the engine that drives the effectiveness of all Vistelar customer service and conflict management tactics. It enables "active intelligence gathering," which drives increased understanding of the other person so you can be more effective at managing conflict and generating non-confrontational outcomes.

A Campus Example

Let us look at an example to see an application of the *Empathy Triad.*

Imagine you are a student and you walk into your school's public safety department after having your car stolen.

You are tired, angry and do not know anything about stolen cars. The officer on duty has dealt with many stolen vehicles, and if she were in your situation, would probably just want to be left alone to investigate the theft on her own. However, that may not be how you want to be treated.

If she is a good officer she will acknowledge you are upset because someone stole your car, acknowledging your perspective. Then, she will try to seek to understand you and your situation so she can see the problem through your eyes. During this process she will discover you know little about how to protect your car from having it stolen.

A Campus Example *continued*

Her goal should be to fully and accurately understand your needs, wants and desires so she can treat you the way you want to be treated. That requires *Empathy.*

Now imagine the officer did a good job and you left the agency in your car because it was recovered while you were talking to the officer. You are a happy customer — right?

Possibly – but possibly not, because the officer did not practice the third element of the *Empathy Triad.* She did not consider what you would be thinking or feeling immediately following the interaction, the next day or later, and therefore, did not adequately anticipate your needs.

As a result, there is a high likelihood that after getting back home, you would be dissatisfied with her service. Here is why: she didn't offer you what you need to prevent your car from being stolen in the future: advice about ignition locking devices, alarms, clubs or whatever.

To summarize:

- A good officer would treat you with dignity by showing respect.
- A better officer would, first, acknowledge your perspective (you are upset because someone stole your car) and then try to seek to understand your needs, wants and desires, so she could treat you the way you want to be treated.
- An outstanding officer would go above and beyond by anticipating your needs (you never want your car stolen again) and offer you advice on how to protect your car from being stolen again in the future.

This individual, by all rights, was a good officer but not an outstanding one because she failed to practice the third element of the *Empathy Triad.* She was probably kicking herself that night for not suggesting a solution to what you were most upset about — having your car stolen and not wanting that to ever happen again.

The Ultimate Goal — Establish A Social Contract

By *Showing Respect*, practicing *Empathy* and applying the conflict management tactics you will learn in this manual, the *Ultimate Goal* of Vistelar's training is to establish a professional *Social Contract* within your agency for how people are to be treated — a voluntary agreement by all employees to consistently treat everyone with dignity by showing respect.

A well-established professional *Social Contract* creates an environment that promotes cooperation, performance excellence and safety, and that is incompatible with emotional and physical violence.

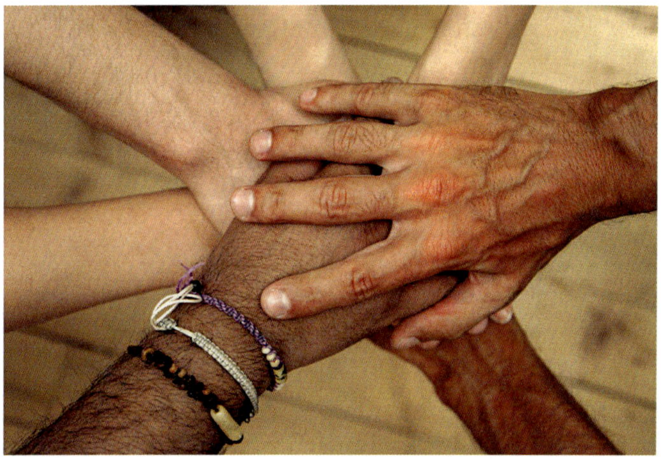

An example of a social contract exists in most libraries, where there is a voluntary agreement to be quiet. It does not matter if you are a business executive, the janitor, or an ex con. If you are making too much noise, the rest of the library patrons know it is OK to "shush" you, and they will do so without hesitation. Then, if that does not work, the library's social contract makes it acceptable for the library staff to get involved and if necessary, request the help of a security officer or the police.

For a professional *Social Contract* to be established, there must be clear expectations for how people should be treated and consistent enforcement of those expectations.

The *Ultimate Goal* of this program is to establish such a *Social Contract* within your agency. If someone – whether it is a citizen or an employee – is being treated poorly, then everyone within the agency is empowered to take the appropriate action. For example, an officer may say something like, "What is going on here? That's not how we treat people around here."

> *"If certain conditions are met and the people inside an organization feel safe among each other, they will work together to achieve things none of them could have ever achieved on their own. [These conditions] create an environment for the free exchange of information and effective communication. This is fundamental to driving innovation, preventing problems from escalating and making organizations better equipped to defend themselves from the outside dangers and to seize the opportunities."*
>
> Simon Sinek, *Leaders Eat Last* (1973 – present)

> *"Inappropriate behavior that goes uncorrected becomes the social norm"*
>
> Joel Lashley, author of *Confidence In Conflict For Healthcare Professionals*

Only when a professional *Social Contract* for how people are to be treated is established can the *Ultimate Goal* of this training to be fully realized within your campus public safety agency

Please Note …

A social contract can also support negative behaviors. We all know of organizations that effectively have a voluntary agreement among employees to act in ways that promote conflict. In such organizations, the journey towards a dignity-driven social contract will obviously take longer.

The positive internal outcomes of establishing a professional *Social Contract* concerning how people are treated can take some time.

SOCIAL CONTRACT

VOLUNTARY AGREEMENT BY ALL EMPLOYEES TO CONSISTENTLY TREAT EVERYONE WITH DIGNITY BY SHOWING RESPECT

Interactions by an agency's public safety professionals with students, campus staff and the general public generally begin and end quickly; therefore, the results, such as increased student and staff satisfaction, cooperation with directions and less injuries, are seen immediately.

In contrast, within the internal operations of an agency, the outcomes of everyone interacting the right way at the point of impact — at meetings, in one-on-one discussions, in the hallway, at lunch, or within teams — takes time to be realized. Each individual interaction has a positive short-term result, but the agency impact, such as increased performance, higher morale, more innovation and lower turnover, is a longer-term proposition.

When effective conflict management is utilized within a campus public safety agency, arguments go from being destructive to productive: people more openly share ideas, conflicts stop being allowed to fester and instead, get resolved, and team efficiency and productivity go up. But, again, all this takes time to be realized.

As a campus public safety professional, you will see the positive results of better conflict management right away in your day-to-day interactions, but to gain the full benefits of developing a professional Social Contract, you will need to have some patience. It will be worth the wait.

Expectation Contracting

At the beginning of Vistelar's instructor-led programs, we go through a process of "expectation contracting" among the instructors and students — with everyone signing onto this agreement:

"We will treat each other with dignity by showing respect, even if we disagree."

The goal of this activity is to start the process of developing a professional *Social Contract* within class.

Over the last 30+ years we have discovered that, for students to learn best, the classroom must be an emotionally and physically safe environment, so that everyone:

- Actively participates without hesitation
- Feels listened to and supported as they share their opinions and attempt new skills
- Offers and accepts supportive feedback

Within a campus public safety agency, expectation contracting, usually initiated by the chief, is the first step on the journey towards establishing a professional *Social Contract.* Once everyone understands the chief's expectations, the next step is for individuals to set an example — "I'm going to treat you with dignity by showing you respect. I ask the same from you".

Then the goal should be to have a majority of campus staff setting that example. When that happens, you are well on your way to having a professional Social Contract for how people are treated embedded in your agency.

Don't Speak Reactively

When interacting with others who are acting badly, especially when negative emotions are being triggered, do not reactively blurt out what first pops into your mind. There are three reasons for this:

1. In the heat of the moment, what you reactively say could unnecessarily escalate a situation. Or, you may make comment you regret or that results in a citizen complaint. As you have probably experienced, people rarely make good decisions when they are angry or frustrated.

2. What you reactively say could be based on ineffective methods or advice you have learned over

time from friends, family members or colleagues, such as:

- Ignore their bad behavior
- Kill them with kindness
- If you say something, you will make things worse
- Defend your ego and save face

Rather than improving a situation, these methods will usually empower a badly-behaving individual to escalate his or her actions.

3. If you speak reactively, you might perform well in one situation and poorly in another, because your natural reactions are not grounded in proven principles. You could be naturally skilled in interacting with others, but because you do not fully understand how and why you do what you do, you may sometimes make mistakes — especially if you are having a bad day. In addition, you will likely struggle to teach others how you do what you do.

BE CONSISTENT IN HOW YOU TREAT PEOPLE

Such inconsistency in addressing bad behavior causes the same problems within an organization that parents discover in dealing with children; it leads to more bad behavior. By not speaking reactively and instead, using the training you will learn in this manual to formulate a response, you will be more consistent in how you treat people.

When interacting with others who are acting badly, don't speak reactively. Instead, consciously pause and then apply the tactics you are learning in this manual.

Please Note ...

Don't Speak Reactively is about what words you use in the heat of the moment. Just saying what naturally pops into your mind (reacting) is almost never the right approach. Instead, you should take a deep breath and thoughtfully respond (see *Be Alert & Decisive*; *Respond, Don't React* and *Showtime Mindset*).

However, "winging it" can work when protecting your personal safety. When out in the world, you should trust your instincts and do not ignore behaviors that give you feelings of uneasiness. If you feel unsafe, be decisive and take the appropriate action to maintain your safety.

Conflict Triggers

Causes of Conflict

Here is a quick summary of what has been covered so far:

- Core Principle: Treat people with dignity by showing respect
- How To Show Respect: Five approaches: see world through their eyes; listen with all senses; ask and explain why; offer options, let them choose; give opportunity to reconsider
- Empathy: Engine that drives the effectiveness of all Vistelar customer service and conflict management tactics, via the *Empathy Triad*
- Social Contract: voluntary agreement by all employees to consistently treat everyone with dignity by showing respect

These are the *Foundations* of effective conflict management.

In this section you will learn the causes of conflict and how to keep it from erupting in you and in others.

Conflict occurs when disagreements or insults escalate, rather than just rolling off a person's back. Why does this happen? Why do differences and slights sometimes affect you negatively and other times don't?

The reason is the presence or absence of *Conflict Triggers*, which can come in the form of spoken words, tone of voice, facial expressions, hand position, body language, posture and physical positioning. When these triggers are present, an interaction that might otherwise be considered routine can escalate to conflict.

There are two main forms of *Conflict Triggers*:

1. Universal triggers, which cause conflict in almost everyone, such as:

- Indignity — from violations to a person's intrinsic value as a human being, such as insults, humiliation or most any action based on prejudice or explicit/implicit bias, which can provoke retaliation or revenge.

  When someone's dignity is violated, the natural reaction is to retaliate or seek revenge. This response is just baked into our DNA because such violations threaten the very essence of who we are, and as you have likely experienced, often remain in our memories forever. Being treated with indignity can cut deeper and fester longer than any physical injury.

- Fear — from emotional or physical threats, often resulting from prejudices, such as gender, race/ethnicity, religion, social class, politics, ideologies, age, disability, sexuality, language, nationality, occupation, education, criminality and physical appearance.

- Stress — from work demands, relationship difficulties, financial problems, emotional disturbances, pain, mental disorders, or being under the influence of drugs or alcohol, which can cause emotional fragility.

CONFLICT TRIGGERS

- UNIVERSAL

- PERSONAL HOT BUTTONS

- Vulnerability — from being viewed as lower in status than others, which can lead to becoming the target of bullying, verbal abuse and threats.

2. Personal triggers, which are unique to you; think of these as your personal hot buttons, such as:
   - Name calling, derogatory remarks
   - Sarcastic tone, dismissive behaviors
   - Eye rolling, inappropriate smiling or laughing
   - Intimidating postures, finger pointing

Please Note ...

Prejudice and bias, whether implicit or explicit, can be a factor within each conflict trigger. Sometimes our prejudices and biases come through (even subconsciously) in your facial expressions, hand position or tone of voice.

For example, if you have a negative bias towards a specific group of people, your feelings towards them may be inadvertently displayed to others through an eye roll or hand gesture. Furthermore, it could seep into your communication via a sarcastic tone.

Please Note ... *continued*

If you apply the core philosophy of this training (show people respect even if you disagree with them) to everyone with whom you interact, your prejudices will be invisible. That invisibility will make it infinitely easier to be effective at conflict management.

"Prejudice is a great time saver. You can form opinions without having to get the facts."
E. B. White, American writer (1899 - 1985)

Conflict Triggers cause people to be more susceptible to conflict, so it is important for you to be aware of yours. With that awareness as a starting point, you can learn how to minimize their impact on you.

Note: societal issues, such as drug abuse, gangs, poverty and poor family functioning, are other *Conflict Triggers*, but are beyond the scope of this training program.

Emotional Equilibrium

When one or more of your *Conflict Triggers* are present in an interaction, your goal should be to minimize their impact on you, so you can keep your cool rather than allowing your reactions to cause a situation to escalate. This is called maintaining your *Emotional Equilibrium.*

Two methods to maintain your *Emotional Equilibrium* are to:

1. Consider that your behavior is likely being caught on camera and, even if it is not, you are always in the public eye.

   With street cameras, body cameras, smart phone cameras and hidden cameras, your "reaction" could end up on YouTube, the evening news, or any social media channel for the whole world to see and forever remember.

   Entire professions are now facing this challenge. For example, as you well know, videos of law enforcement incidents are in the news almost every day. Internet and news media do not cover the millions of good police interactions but will broadcast anything bad that happens.

2. Consider the situation of the other person — practice *Empathy*

   Put yourself in the other person's shoes. Is it possible he or she is activating your personal triggers inadvertently or as a response to something else going on in his or her life? When *Empathy* is deeply practiced, being angry with anyone becomes quite difficult.

Either of these two considerations should have a calming effect on your emotions.

Another effective way to maintain your *Emotional Equilibrium* is to build *Trigger Guards*. Here is how:

a. Define them — as stated previously, be aware of your *Conflict Triggers*

b. Name them — label your *Conflict Triggers*, so that you can acknowledge them.

   For example, as a police officer you might have a *Conflict Trigger* of being asked, "Want a donut?" – so he would label that trigger as "Mr. Donut."

c. Own them — take responsibility for how you respond to *Conflict Triggers*

   For example, when faced with a "Want-a-donut" question, you would say to yourself, "Ah, another Mr. Donut" and move on, rather than taking it personally.

Building *Trigger Guards* creates an internal warning system to alert you when you are in danger of allowing your *Emotional Equilibrium* to become disrupted so you can pause and thoughtfully respond rather than impulsively react.

An additional method to maintain your *Emotional Equilibrium* is to consider whom you represent, such as your family, coworkers, employer, community, or even the entire campus public safety profession.

Despite how you might feel inside, your goal should be to keep your ego out of the situation and not show a negative reaction.

You are in control of how you respond to the behavior of others. Be aware of your *Conflict Triggers* and take personal responsibility for them, with the goal of maintaining your *Emotional Equilibrium*.

MAINTAIN YOUR EMOTIONAL EQUILIBRIUM

- **REALIZE YOU'RE LIKELY BEING RECORDED**
- **PRACTICE EMPATHY**
- **BUILD TRIGGER GUARDS**
- **CONSIDER WHO YOU REPRESENT**

The Word on the Street: Emotional Equilibrium

Being a generally calm and even keeled person, I had a hard time identifying a *Conflict Trigger* when I was first introduced to the concept back in 2012. But then one night, while on patrol, I got a lesson of a lifetime. It was about 3am and a monster storm with tornadic wind and rain was headed towards campus. Many of our officers, including myself, were running ragged to get pedestrians off of the street and to help the homeless find shelter. In the middle of the chaos I looked up and saw a very elderly gentleman struggling in his wheelchair – he was stuck in the street, just spinning his wheels against the flooded curb.

The Word on the Street: Emotional Equilibrium *continued*

I ran out of my squad car in torrential rain to help the man, and I was able to free him from his puddle and push him back up the block to his home. What happened next was a moment I will never forget. As I asked the man if he was going to be OK for the night, he slowly turned his chair around, looking at the ground. He slowly looked up at me from under his WWII veteran's cap and then he scathed, "I have no, absolutely no respect for you. A woman. You have no business being in law enforcement." And then he slowly turned around, and entered his home.

I remember standing there speechless. Jaw on the floor. Blood boiling. Dripping rain from head to toe, under my vest and through all of my gear. Furious.

I stood there dumbfounded, I was trying to think of all the witty and horrible things I could quip back at the man that could possibly help repair my damaged ego. But it was in that moment that I finally understood the concept of a *Conflict Trigger.* Something that someone says to you that will set you off, ring your bell, and make your blood boil. Those are the triggers you are looking to identify, label, and protect yourself from, so that they don't catch you off guard in the future causing you to say or do something that you will regret forever!

- Lt. Jill Weisensel, M.S.

Triggers of Others

Now that you are aware of your *Conflict Triggers* and know how to maintain your *Emotional Equilibrium*, realize that others have *Conflict Triggers* of their own.

To prevent conflict — with students, staff, faculty, other officers, your supervisor, friends, family or whoever — you must be careful your spoken words, tone of voice, facial expressions, hand position, body language, posture or physical positioning do not set off the *Conflict Triggers* of others.

Reflect on your own *Conflict Triggers* and consider these additional possibilities:

- Use of profanities
- Facial expressions that could be interpreted as disapproval
- Body postures that may communicate superiority
- Pointing of the "parental" finger
- Lecturing in an authoritarian manner
- Ordering, moralizing, blaming, shaming, arguing, criticizing, lying
- Use of a sarcastic or condescending tone of voice
- Veiled or explicit threats
- Eye rolling or sighing
- Any indication of prejudice
- Any violations of a person's dignity

If a situation requires you to assert yourself, such as to get your needs met or to address a violation of your dignity, use "I statements" instead of "You statements" that may come across as blaming or judgmental.

If a situation requires you to assert yourself, such as to get your needs met or to address a violation of your dignity, use "I statements" instead of "You statements" that may come across as blaming or judgmental.

You statement: "You are rude to cut in in line"

I statement: "I believe I was next in line"

In your "I statements," avoid using:

- Inflammatory words, such as fail, neglect, ignore — always, never, constantly — frequently, often, repeatedly
- Victim words, such as hurt, disappointed or let down
- Explanations as to why you need to assert yourself — keep your comments focused on the other person's behavior
- Exaggerations of the impact of the other person's behavior on you
- Excessive repetition — assert yourself confidently one or two times to let your feelings be known and then move on

In addition, realize there are some things you should just never say because most people will react negatively. Here are some examples of what not to say, with an alternative in parentheses:

- "Calm down" (alternative: "Can you explain what's happening?")
- "I know just how you must feel" (alternative: "That must be very difficult for you.")
- "I need you to do this for me" (alternative: "Would you please?")
- "What is your problem?" (alternative: "What can I do to help?)
- "You people" (alternative: "Will everyone please …")

You can prevent a lot of conflict by being careful to not set off the *Conflict Triggers* of individuals with whom you interact. Realize that most others have not likely been trained on how to maintain their *Emotional Equilibrium*.

Rewind Button

In managing conflict with another person, be aware that each person has his or her own personal conflict triggers that you may set off. If you inadvertently activate someone's trigger, the simplest and best response is to apologize and ask to start over. We call this pushing the *Rewind Button*.

If you clearly do something wrong, do not hesitate to apologize. As a contact professional, you are not apologizing for doing your job; you are simply acknowledging and expressing regret for your mistake. Making an apology does not weaken your authority — in fact, it makes you appear stronger by showing you are not afraid to be human and consider the feelings of others.

TRIGGERS OF OTHERS

- **BODY LANGUAGE**
- **PHYSICAL POSITIONING**
- **HAND PLACEMENT**
- **POSTURE**
- **FACIAL EXPRESSIONS**
- **TONE OF VOICE**
- **SPOKEN WORDS**

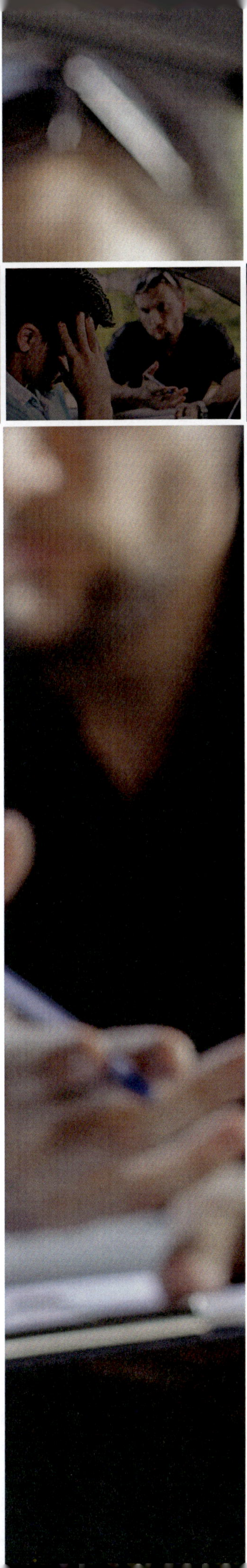

6 C's of Conflict Management

Vistelar's training focuses on addressing the entire spectrum of human conflict at the point of impact from before an interaction begins through to the consequences of how an interaction is managed.

"Point of impact" is the short period of time when disagreements, insults or gateway behaviors, like swearing or aggressive posturing, can escalate to conflict and on to emotional and/or physical violence. Effective point-of-impact conflict management using Vistelar's methodologies ensures the best possible outcome for interactions with others and sets the stage for positive future interactions.

Vistelar's methodologies are not meant to address longer-term situations, such as ongoing relationship difficulties or lengthy negotiations. However, many of the principles and tactics you'll learn will have a positive impact on such situations.

Vistelar's 6 C's of Conflict Management: *Point-Of-Impact Conflict Management Framework*™ provides a means to analyze interactions and determine which conflict management tactic should be used in which phase of an interaction.

The blue boxes in the graphic below describe the three elements of all interactions:

- **Context**: Approach considerations prior to an interaction, such as assessment of risk and physical positioning, decision on whether to proceed and personal mindset.
- **Contact**: Interaction considerations, such as words used, tone of voice, facial expressions, eye contact, hand position, body language and posture.
- **Closure**: Follow-through considerations, such as ensuring the situation is stabilized, summarizing decisions, and reviewing the interaction.

The primary goals of these elements are non-escalation (conflict prevention), achieving the best possible outcome and establishing a positive foundation for any future interactions.

The red boxes in the graphic describe what can happen when interactions escalate:

- **Conflict**: When questioning, anger or verbal abuse enters into an interaction.
- **Crisis**: When the person with whom you are interacting is displaying at-risk behaviors.
- **Combat**: When resistance or aggression results in physical engagement initiated by either party.

The primary goals in the face of *Conflict*, *Crisis*, or *Combat* are de-escalation, everyone's safety, and shifting the situation to a positive outcome.

Note that all interactions have a *Context*, *Contact* and *Closure* element but only some interactions progress to *Conflict*, *Crisis* and/or *Combat.*

"Our job is to keep people on the blue brick road and off the red brick road."

Derrick S. Washington, Sr., retired Lieutenant, Milwaukee County Sheriff's Office

The "blue brick road" (the blue boxes) is where we want to keep an interaction. We certainly don't want to be the initiator of it moving to the "red brick road" (the red boxes). The only way an interaction should ever get on the "red brick road" is if others take us there. When that happens, getting back on the "blue brick road" should be the goal.

Also note that the need to analyze an interaction before it begins is especially important relative to use-of-force incidents and situations of officer-created jeopardy.

Systemized Structure of Tactics

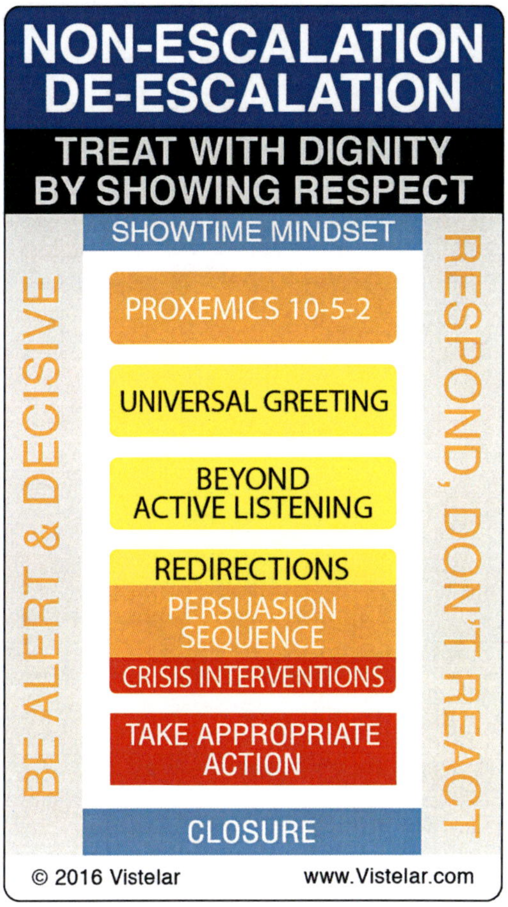

Vistelar has created a *Systemized Structure Of Tactics*, outlined in this graphic, which makes our methodologies easy to learn, remember, apply and teach.

The remainder of this manual focuses on teaching the "how-tos" of each of the tactics listed.

Prior to getting started with this training, here is a brief orientation to this graphic.

Treat With Dignity By Showing Respect is listed first to highlight this core principle of customer service and conflict management.

Be Alert & Decisive and *Respond, Don't React* are located on the sides to emphasize that these tactics should be considered at all times prior to and during an interaction.

Showtime Mindset is listed next to indicate that this tactic should be applied in advance of any interaction.

The above tactics as well as *Proxemics 10-5-2*, *Universal Greeting* and *Beyond Active Listening* are non-escalation tactics, with the goal of predicting and preventing conflict, and if necessary, turning a defensive atmosphere into a supportive one.

Redirections, *Persuasion Sequence* and *Crisis Interventions* are de-escalation tactics with the goal of recovering from a conflict or crisis situation.

Take Appropriate Action and *Closure* are ending-an-interaction tactics.

Closure is at the bottom of the graphic to indicate that this tactic should always be the final step of any interaction.

Here is a numerical listing of the eleven tactics:

1. Treat With Dignity By Showing Respect
2. Be Alert & Decisive; Respond, Don't React
3. Showtime Mindset
4. Proxemics 10-5-2
5. Universal Greeting
6. Beyond Active Listening
7. Redirections
8. Persuasion Sequence
9. Crisis Interventions
10. Take Appropriate Action
11. Closure

The graphic to the right provides a reminder of the details of some of these eleven tactics.

HOW TO SHOW PEOPLE RESPECT

See World Through Their Eyes
Listen With All Senses
Ask and Explain Why
Offer Options, Let Them Choose
Give Opportunity To Reconsider

UNIVERSAL GREETING

Appropriate Greeting
Name & Affiliation
Reason For Contact
Relevant Question

DE-ESCALATIONS

Empathize: Clarify - Paraphrase - Reflect Mirror - Advocate - Summarize

Redirect: Acknowledge → Back To Issue

Persuade: 1) Explain Why 2) Offer Options 3) Give Opportunity To Reconsider

Crisis Management: Reduce Stimulation Separate & Support - Adapt Communication Meet Urgent Unmet Needs

Courses
Conflict Management For:
Gatekeeper Staff - Contact Professionals - Crisis First Responders

VISTELAR *Addressing The Entire Spectrum Of Human Conflict*

Non-Escalation

Review and What's Next

So far you have learned the foundations of Vistelar's conflict management system:

- Conflict is inevitable
- Conflict can have positive or negative outcomes depending on how well it is managed
- Vistelar's *Core Principle, Five Approaches to Showing Respect, Empathy Triad* and *The Ultimate Goal*
- Importance of not speaking reactively

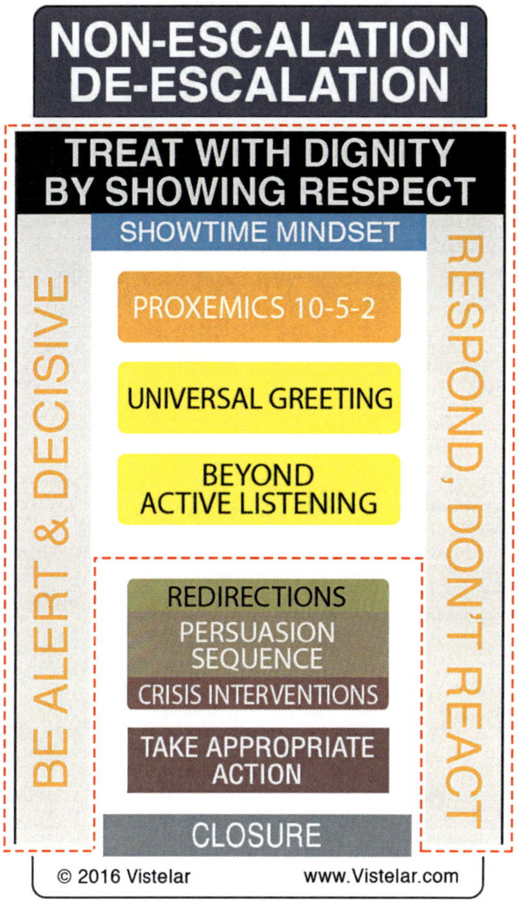

You have also learned about *Conflict Triggers*: yours, how to maintain your *Emotional Equilibrium* and how to not set off the triggers of others.

Finally, you have been introduced to Vistelar's *Point-Of-Impact Conflict Management Framework*™ and *Systemized Structure of Tactics.*

Next, non-escalation tactics will be discussed — tactics focused on predicting and preventing conflict and, if necessary, turning a defensive atmosphere into a supportive one. These tactics include:

- *Treat With Dignity By Showing Respect*

- *Be Alert & Decisive; Respond, Don't React*
- *Showtime Mindset*
- *Proxemics 10-5-2*
- *Universal Greeting*
- *Beyond Active Listening*

In addition, practicing these tactics will improve your relationships with students, campus staff, colleagues, your supervisors, friends and family and enhance your confidence to deal with conflict head-on, rather than shying away from it.

These tactics are used primarily during the *Context* and *Contact* elements of an interaction.

> *"Think how much time you could save if you spent more time on non-escalation versus working on de-escalation after the contact escalated"*
>
> Gary T. Klugiewicz, VDI Director of Training

Framework: Context and Contact

In this section, you will learn Vistelar's non-escalation tactics — those that apply to these two elements of Vistelar's 6 C's of Conflict Management: *Point-Of-Impact Conflict Management Framework*™.

Context: Approach considerations prior to an interaction, such as assessment of risk and physical positioning, decision on whether to proceed, and personal mindset.

Goal: prepare for the interaction

Contact: Interaction considerations, such as words used, tone of voice, facial expressions, eye contact, hand position, body language and posture.

Primary Goal: non-escalation to prevent conflict and begin on a positive note

Secondary Goal: turn a defensive atmosphere into a supportive one

As you progress through this section, consider how the non-escalation tactics you are learning apply to these first two elements of an interaction.

1. Treat With Dignity By Showing Respect

Treat People With Dignity By Showing Respect. is the core principle of customer service and conflict management and serves as the foundation of everything Vistelar teaches.

Treating people with dignity is an acknowledgement showing respect is how you treat people with dignity.

Here is a review of how to show people respect:

1. See world through their eyes
2. Listen with all senses
3. Ask and explain why
4. Offer options, let them choose
5. Give opportunity to reconsider

Empathy is the engine that drives the effectiveness of all Vistelar customer service and conflict management tactics, which is accomplished by applying the *Empathy Triad:*

- Acknowledge their perspective
- Seek to understand
- Anticipate their needs

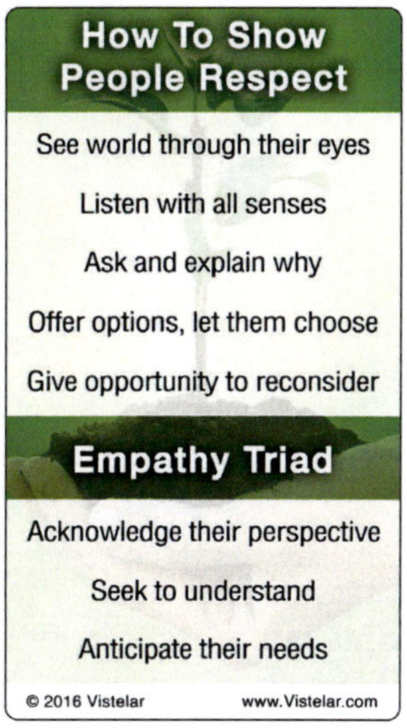

2. Be Alert & Decisive | Respond, Don't React

At all times when out in the world but especially when on patrol, pay attention to your surroundings and be ready to take action if you sense a safety risk, either from emotional or physical violence (*Be Alert & Decisive*). Then, when verbal or physical action is necessary, thoughtfully respond rather than impulsively react (*Respond, Don't React*).

As explained in the original *Street Survival Seminar:* 1) if you are not paying attention, you will never see the assault coming. The great equalizer in life is getting hit with a baseball bat from the blind side; 2) if you are not decisive and willing to make a decision, you have given control of the situation to the other person; and 3) if you have not planned and practiced your response, your response is a fantasy that could rapidly turn into a tragedy. If you haven't practiced your plan, you do not know if it will work in real world applications.

"Warning: proper response requires that you: 1) remain alert; 2) be decisive; 3) have a preplanned, practiced response in mind."

Gary T. Klugiewicz, VDI Director of Training

Implicit Bias

The *Respond, Don't React* tactic keeps you safe but there is also evidence it can prevent people from acting on their implicit biases.

Even well-meaning people frequently harbor hidden prejudices[7]. Studies have shown these subtle biases are widespread and associated with discrimination in legal, economic, and organizational settings.

Recent research[8] suggests that people have the capacity to override their worst instincts — if they are able to reflect on their decision-making as opposed to acting on their first impulse.

> *"When people made their decisions swiftly — in a few seconds or less — they were biased in their punishment decisions. Not only did they punish out-group members more harshly, they also treated members of their own group more leniently. But we also found that people could overcome these biased instincts if they engaged in rational deliberation. When people had the chance to reflect on their decision, they were largely unbiased, handing out equal punishments to in-group and out-group members."*

Daniel A. Yudkin and Jay Van Bavel
The Roots of Implicit Bias, *The New York Times*, Dec. 9, 2016

This attention to your surroundings (*Be Alert*) – in all directions – is called *540 Degree Proxemic Management* and is a situational awareness strategy. Later in this manual you will learn Vistelar's *Proxemics 10-5-2* conflict management tactic, but in this section, we want to introduce you to the concept of proxemics.

Proxemics is the study of the human use of space: how distance, relative positioning and hand placement affect how people communicate with each other. To be effective at conflict management, you must constantly *Be Alert* to the proxemics of a situation. This includes considering:

- Your distance from other people or physical hazards (greater distance equals additional time and additional time equals more options)
- Your position within a 360-degree arc of other people (relative positioning)
- What is happening above you (the other 180 degrees)
- Sight lines (your uninhibited line of sight)
- Barrier options, such as tables, chairs, corners, hills, ditches and garbage cans
- Exit opportunities
- Your hand placement

Being Alert of all of these considerations (*540 Degree Proxemic Management*) impacts both your personal safety and how others perceive you.

Important Note

The concepts of target hardening and crime prevention through environmental design ("designing out crime") also fall within the realm of *540 Degree Proxemic Management.*

Many high-risk crime areas can be evaluated and redesigned to reduce the level of threat the area presents to the community. By assessing an area for vulnerabilities, measures can be taken to reduce those vulnerabilities, and therefore, particular risks within that environment, think of the design and layout of many medieval castles. They weren't designed with rock walls, large towers, draw-bridge entries, and moats simply for aesthetic purposes. Those design elements were added over time to ensure the castle was fortified and less vulnerable to attack. The high walls and lookout towers kept intruders out of the castle while also providing clear sight lines for a long distance (allowing natural surveillance), and a draw bridge allowed for access control.

"The physical environment can be manipulated to produce behavioral effects which will reduce crime."

Timothy D. Crowe

Now that you have a basic understanding of proxemics, here are some specific tactics on how to *Be Alert & Decisive*:

- Constantly scan your environment with as many senses as you can. You should be listening and visually scanning several seconds ahead of where you are going, and try not to be distracted by phones or other technology. The more distracted you are within your environment, the more vulnerable you are to it.

  "You can observe a lot by just watching."

  Yogi Berra, American professional baseball player and coach (1925 - 2015)

  Being aware of a verbal or physical threat, even seconds in advance, may keep you safe by giving you time to act instead of react.

- Do not ignore behaviors that give you feelings of uneasiness. If you feel unsafe, be decisive and either do not enter, or if appropriate for the situation, leave. Trust your intuition.

  "Never discredit your gut instinct. You're not paranoid. Your body can pick up on bad vibrations. If something deep inside of you says something is not right about a person or situation, trust it."

  Spirit Science

GATEWAYS TO VIOLENCE

- ANTISOCIAL ACTIONS

- VEILED THREATS

- OVERT THREATS

- VIOLENCE

- Practice "when-then thinking" (a concept developed by Vistelar advisor, Coach Bob Lindsey) — plan what you will do "when" a verbal or physical incident happens, rather than thinking "if this happens, then I will ..."

  You should have a preplanned, practice response to situations where conflict could occur and decide in advance your plan of action should things escalate. Your plan should include verbal tactics, escape routes, how to get help, and physical alternatives.

- Consider level of risk (e.g., presence of weapons) and be aware of threat indicators, signals that your safety may be compromised because the communication with another person is breaking down. The most important indicators to watch for are the other person's:
  - Inability to manage distance, which is a reflection of your and the other person's safety and comfort level
  - Failure to control position, which is an indicator of the other person's respect or disrespect towards you
  - Tone of voice / word choice / excessive repetition, which is an indicator of the other person's frustration and anger
  - Hand movement, which is an indicator of the other person's ability to take action
  - Eye focus, which is an indicator of the other person's intent
- Be aware of gateway behaviors, a concept developed by Joel Lashley, author of *Confidence In Conflict For Healthcare Professionals*, which are antisocial actions that might not make you feel threatened at the moment, but have been shown to be reliable predictors of violence. Examples include: yelling, cursing, name-calling, verbal disrespect, aggressive posturing and veiled threats. Note this possible progression: antisocial actions ➔ veiled threats ➔ overt threats ➔ violence.
- Assigning a color code (originated by Jeff Cooper, internationally known firearms instructor) to situations can be helpful in assuming the appropriate level of caution.

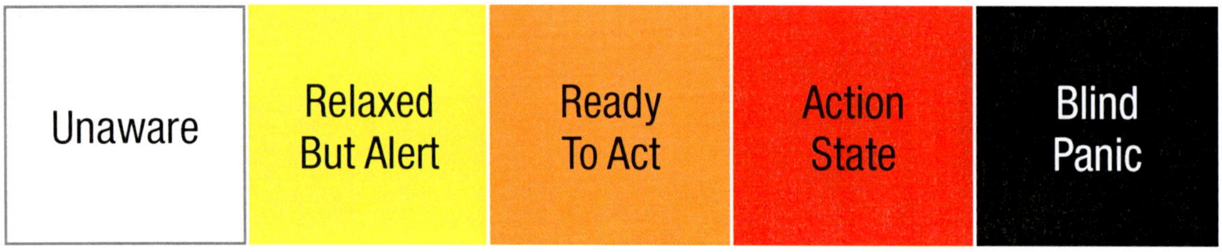

Other than within the safety of your own home, never assign a color below yellow; you should not ever be totally oblivious to what is going on around you.

- Practice this tactic, so beyond just having the knowledge as to what to do, you also have the skills and abilities to *Be Alert & Decisive — Respond, Don't React* in the face of both verbal and physical threats and incidents.

Ethical Intervention

We are all human. Every now and then, we may have a bad day. Personal stress, lack of sleep, kids, our working work environment, and financial troubles can all wear our patience thin.

Be Alert & Decisive; Respond, Don't React apply to when you see a partner or colleague heading in a direction or, perhaps, taking an action he or she will likely regret or will get him or her into trouble.

In such circumstances, you have an obligation to step in, "tap out" your partner or colleague (verbally or physically) and take over the interaction — to execute an Ethical Intervention. As a contact professional, your job is to keep everyone safe: verbally if you can, physically if you must.

If you ignore their actions, you are condoning them.

> *"Officers should be obligated to intervene when they believe another officer is about to use excessive or unnecessary force, or when they witness colleagues using excessive or unnecessary force, or engaging in other misconduct."*
>
> *PERF: 30 Guiding Principles On Use Of Force* — March 2016

When faced with such situations, all of the *Be Alert & Decisive* and *Respond, Don't React* strategies apply: situational awareness, being attentive to gateway behaviors and threat indicators, when-then thinking, assigning a color code, and thoughtfully responding rather than impulsively reacting.

3. Showtime Mindset

In advance of any interaction where you anticipate or are faced with conflict, whether in person or on the phone, establish a *Showtime Mindset.* Imagine yourself stepping onto a stage to give a performance.

- Clear your mind of whatever else might be going on in your life, put aside any negative feelings or prejudices
- Focus all your attention on your audience
- Get all elements of communication — words, non-verbals and paraverbals (see below) — in alignment with the situation.
- Act as if other people are your equal, no matter who they are

Here are the specific steps to establish a *Showtime Mindset*:

1. Say to yourself, "It's *Showtime*!"
2. Stack your blocks; adopt an assertive posture
3. Take a deep breath through your nose, pause, and blow the breath out through your mouth
4. Put on the appropriate facial expression for the situation
5. Use positive self-talk — say to yourself, "I've got this."
6. Step onto the stage

Note: with the prevalence of video cameras, every interaction is likely being recorded. Therefore, from the moment you leave home, stepping onto a stage does not need to be imagined — it is actually real. It really is "*Showtime*."

Please Note ...

In very stressful situations, the third step in the *Showtime Mindset* sequence can be accentuated with autogenic breathing — a technique used to minimize the effects of the body's "fight or flight" mechanism. Here are the steps:

- Breath in for a count of 3
- Hold breath for a count of 3
- Exhale for a count of 3
- Repeat as needed — paying attention to your inhaling and exhaling — until your *Emotional Equilibrium* is under control

Effective use of the *Showtime Mindset* tactic requires all elements of communication to be in alignment with the situation. Just like an actor on stage, your words, paraverbals (tone of voice, pace, pitch, modulation) and non-verbals (facial expressions, eye contact, hand position, body language, posture and physical positioning) must all send the same message.

"Since you never get a second chance to make a first impression, remember to control your body language and facial expressions."

Dave Young, Arma Director of Training

And, as you've probably discovered, your non-verbals and paraverbals are almost always far more important to the message you convey as the words you speak. As you've probably heard, "It's not what you say, it's how you say it."

This is especially true in the midst of conflict. For example:

- You cannot overcome non-verbals that express lack of confidence, such as avoiding eye contact, slouching and looking anxious, with confident-sounding words and tone of voice.
- You cannot overcome threatening non-verbals, like staring, toe-to-toe positioning and aggressive posturing, with calm-sounding words and tone of voice.

More On Paraverbals

Using the right words is important, but your non-verbals and paraverbals are often the primary driver of the outcome. That is why establishing a *Showtime Mindset* is an essential starting point for all interactions where you anticipate or are faced with conflict, with students, with campus staff, within your agency and in your personal life.

Relative to paraverbals, tone of voice is usually the most important. The tone inflected on a sentence imparts on the listener the attitude of the speaker, whether the speaker intended to or not. Quite often, people will hear and remember the tone of what was being said far longer than what was actually said. Two of the most dangerous tones to use (the ones that can anger people easily) are sarcasm and condescension.

However, the other paraverbals of pace, pitch, modulation are also important.

Pace is the rate at which you speak. The average person speaks conversationally at a rate of about 110-150 words per minute. Speaking at a slower rate could cause people to lose interest in what you're saying or be perceived as a lack of confidence. Conversely, speaking at a faster rate faster could be perceived as scared or panicky.

Pitch is the highness or lowness of voice, like the "key" on a piano. A high pitch can be perceived as anxious, whereas a lower pitch sounds more authoritative.

Modulation is the variation of pitch in voice. Speaking with little modulation can be perceived as uninteresting and prevents the delivery of inflection on important points.

To better understand the concept of paraverbals, try reading the following sentences out loud by placing specific emphasis on the underlined word:

- "I didn't say you were a bad driver." (Implying I didn't say it, but someone else did)
- "I didn't say you were stupid." (Implying I may have communicated it another way)
- "I didn't say you were old." (Implying I may have said or meant something else entirely)

The Word on the Street: Showtime Success

As a police supervisor, I use the *Showtime Mindset* tactic nearly every day. I often find myself in the middle of competing demands while also managing multiple personnel issues.

As a supervisor, I have to set the tone for my shift. My demeanor should serve as a thermostat, rather than a thermometer, because if I'm having a bad day I could easily cast a storm cloud over the entire crew. The *Showtime Mindset* is one tactic I use to ensure I am the calm and collected supervisor others need and expect of me, even if I'm paddling like crazy and being pulled in several directions under the surface.

I sometimes say that I am more firefighter than police officer because I so often find myself putting out "fires." One day, while in the middle of several tasks and approaching deadlines faster than I could count them, I was dispatched to a walk-in parent complaint in the lobby. I remember being instantly frustrated that I had to stop what I was doing, and I could feel that I was in a really impatient mood.

The Word on the Street: Showtime Success *continued*

Recognizing that, I used the *Showtime Mindset* tactic by pausing, taking several deep breaths and clearing my head. Even though I didn't know the nature of the complaint, I told myself that I could handle it, and I stood up straight, walked into the lobby, and confidently looked the parent in the eye while shaking their hand, and introduced myself using the *Universal Greeting* (which you will learn later in this manual). By doing all of those things I prepared myself professionally and put my best foot forward. By using the appropriate facial expression, word choice, and tone, I was able to instill confidence in the parent that I was competent and there to address the concern-setting the stage for a successful customer-service oriented interaction.

- Lt. Jill Weisensel, M.S.

Please Note ...

'Much of 'spoken' communication is actually non-verbal in nature. Facial expressions and gestures, and vocal elements such as 'tone of voice' can be equally important to the words that are said. In many situations, the listener trusts and believes the non-verbal cues more than the actual words. Understanding these non-verbal elements can make police officers more effective in communicating, which can help to de-escalate volatile situations."

PERF: Integrating Communications, Assessment, and Tactics Training Guide For Diffusing Critical Incidents October 2016

Relative to step #4 — "Put on the appropriate facial expression for the situation" — you need dozens of faces to draw upon (not just one stock face) so you can select the best one to harmonize with the goal at hand: e.g., pleasant, sad, calm, stern.

In law enforcement, words are considered a "force option" available to officers. If you truly embrace that concept and recognize professional dialogue as an intervention option, then you can see how an "eye roll" could be considered escalatory, and therefore, a possible misuse of force. Dialogue, or an officer's ability to speak on the street, is often overlooked as a fundamental skill. Dialogue is actually an officer's safest and most used tactic, and your most effective street communicators will be those officers who can maximize their word choice and paraverbal delivery.

Please Note ...

While *Showtime Mindset* is primarily a face-to-face interaction tactic, it also has application when communicating by telephone. While people cannot "see" the results of steps #2 and #4 (assertive posture, appropriate facial expression), they can certainly "feel" the results.

Do not think for a moment that, when on the telephone, your non-verbals do not come across loud and clear.

Another way to think about *Showtime Mindset* is to consider what math symbol is floating over your head when you begin interacting with another person, a technique originated by Vistelar advisor Master Chan Lee. Our. Our non-verbals communicate messages to other people long before we ever open our mouths. In any given interaction, in relationship to the other person, ask yourself: Do you look (your non-verbals) less-than (< : passive), greater-than (> : aggressive) or equal-to (= : assertive)?

To be effective at conflict management, the equal-to (= : assertive) symbol is what you are after. You do not want to look (your non-verbals) or sound (your paraverbals) passive or aggressive to the other person; you want to appear as his or her confident equal.

Projecting and sounding confident, as if you are the other person's equal, gives you the best chance of starting an interaction on a positive note. If you come across as greater-than, the other person will likely get defensive and become less receptive to communication or cooperation. In law enforcement and campus safety this is somewhat difficult to overcome because you wear a uniform which projects authority and a position of power. You can counterbalance this by projecting appropriate non-verbal mannerisms and softening your tone.

To drive home this point in our youth anti-bullying programs, we get the kids on their feet and have them yell out these lines in unison.

- You are how you sound!
- You are what you project!
- You are how you respond! *(Respond, Don't React)*

What we have found is that kids are not bullied due to some personal characteristic, like weight, race or sexual orientation. Instead, it is because others perceive them as vulnerable, as having a less-than (<) symbol floating over their head. Sometimes, just teaching a bullied child to have a *Showtime Mindset* is enough to cause the bullying to stop.

Just like the kids in our anti-bullying programs, your goal should be to appear as the confident equal of the person with whom you are interacting. You might try repeating the phrases above to yourself to get accustomed to having a *Showtime Mindset.*

Your Team Is Watching

If you are a leader within your organization, realize your team members are watching you carefully and all the time. They are constantly trying to figure out which employees you favor or do not favor, which ideas you support or are against, which team behaviors you value, and the nature of your *Conflict Triggers*. They are paying attention to every little thing you do: what you say, your words, non-verbals and paraverbals — everything. So, when interacting with your team, remember it is always *Showtime*!

4. Proxemics 10-5-2

As discussed earlier in this manual, proxemics is the study of the human use of space.

Your physical presence — distance, relative positioning and hand placement — affect the comfort level of people interacting with you and your personal safety, whether you are dealing with students, campus staff, colleagues, friends or family members.

To be effective with proxemics:

- Be respectful of other people's personal space: the area which, if encroached upon, causes most individuals to feel discomfort, anxiety or anger. This distance varies by culture, but generally is two to four feet. Do not get too close without asking permission.
- When approaching people, introduce yourself from an appropriate distance and ask permission before coming closer (see *10-5-2* below).
- Stand at an angle to another person rather than directly in front of him or her. This position is less threatening and enables you to more easily escape if there is a safety concern.
- Maintain distance and positioning that prevents another person from ever being able to attack you from behind. The best way to never have someone grab your hair or put you in a rear chokehold is to never put yourself in a position where such an attack is possible. For example, when guiding a person to another location, always follow the person with your hands up rather than allowing him or her to follow you.
- When in close proximity to someone, keep your hand placement above your waist with open palms. This is a signal of honesty, indicates you are not hiding something and is a better hand position from which to block a physical attack.

PROXEMICS 10-5-2

- DISTANCE
- RELATIVE POSITIONING
- HAND PLACEMENT

Relative to the distance element of proxemics, there are three points where you should evaluate the risk level before moving closer, whether you are approaching a person or he or she is approaching you.

Relative to the distance element of proxemics, there are three points where you should evaluate the risk level before moving closer, whether you are approaching a person or he or she is approaching you.

- 10 Feet: Evaluation / Exit — At this distance, if you do not feel safe or are not prepared to become involved, you are far enough away to completely avoid the situation. Alternatively, you can deliberately decide to move closer.
- 5 Feet: Communication / Evade — At this distance, if the situation still seems safe, you are close enough to begin a verbal interaction, with an emphasis on listening with all your senses. Alternatively, you can flee.
- 2 Feet: Operation / Escape — At this distance, you are actively operating in the situation, but if things go badly, you must be prepared to escape.

In our live classes, we teach and practice a series of proxemic tactics that represent the application of the above principles. Below are pictured some of these tactics.

One-hand stop sign

Two-hand stop sign

Emergency timeout

Thinker stance

Guiding hands

Tactical sitting

5. Universal Greeting

When you first interact with someone — especially if you are a person of authority — these four questions generally pop into people's heads:

1. Who are you?
2. What gives you your authority?
3. Why are you interacting with me?
4. What's in it for me?

If you do not immediately answer these questions, the other person will often:

- Feel inhibited from communicating with you
- Fill in the blanks with incorrect answers, such as misidentification as to who you are; assumption you believe he or she is doing something wrong; or expectation the interaction is going to take a long time
- Feel disrespected

Any of these outcomes could cause an interaction to start on a negative note or even escalate. The *Universal Greeting* tactic prevents these outcomes. It has four steps:

1. **Appropriate greeting**
2. **Name and affiliation**
3. **Reason for contact**
4. **Relevant question**

Here is an example:

"Good morning.
I'm Officer Jones with the the Campus Public Safety.
The reason I approached you is because you look lost.
May I help you?"

For the delivery, just like with *Showtime Mindset,* make sure all elements of communication — words, non-verbals and paraverbals — are in alignment with the situation. Speak calmly and in a moderate volume. Do not respond to a raised voice by raising your own voice. Put on the appropriate facial expression for the situation. Adopt a non-threatening posture and hand position.

The *Universal Greeting* explains who you are, your source of authority and the reason for your contact, and then encourages the other person to talk. This a) establishes a positive initial contact, b) develops rapport and c) is the ultimate in showing respect. Then, through listening with all your senses to his or her answer to your relevant question, it gives you an opportunity to learn more about this person: active intelligence gathering.

If you already know the other person, still use this greeting but add his or her name to Step #1 and skip step #2 ("Good morning Bob. The reason I …").

You should move deliberately through the four steps to not delay giving the other person a chance to talk. Only then, should you deal with other matters, such as providing further explanation, giving an estimate of expected duration, asking for identification or answering his or her additional questions.

The *Universal Greeting* is called this for a reason: it is universal. You should use it to begin almost any encounter: with students, with faculty & staff, within your agency and in your personal life.

Here are some additional examples:

UNIVERSAL GREETING

- APPROPRIATE GREETING
- NAME AND AFFILIATION
- REASON FOR CONTACT
- RELEVANT QUESTION

Professional

"Good evening.
I'm Officer Jones with Campus Public Safety.
The reason I'm here is because we received a call about loud music.
Would it be possible to lower the volume?

"Good afternoon.
I'm Officer Jones and this is Officer Smith with the University Police.
The reason we stopped by is because we received a call reporting a suspicious person walking through the area looking into car windows.
Have you seen anyone doing this?

Within Your Institution

"Good Afternoon.
My name is Tony Martinez and I'm an officer with campus safety.
The reason I'm calling is that I'd like to reserve a technology capable room for our in-service next week.
Can we please schedule a meeting to discuss availability and equipment?"

"Good Afternoon.
My name is John Smith and I'm a campus public safety officer.
The reason I wanted to talk with you is because I heard shouting from this hallway.
Is everyone all right?"

In Your Personal Life

"Good Afternoon.
My name is Sue Carpenter and I am the mother of Evan who is in your 5th grade class.
The reason I'm calling is because I am concerned Evan is being picked on in class.
Do you have a few minutes to talk about how we can keep Evan safe at school?"

"Good Afternoon Officer.
My name is Dave Johnson and I'm a student at Springfield College.
The reason I'm here is my friend to pick me up after soccer practice.
Can you get me in to assist you?"

"Good Afternoon.
My name is Angie Lee and I'm a public safety officer at the local college.
This is my first time at this event.
How are you folks doing?"

Please Note ...

The *Universal Greeting* is just as applicable in written communications as in verbal. When writing a letter or email, always start with the four steps: an appropriate greeting, your name and affiliation, the reason for your contact and a relevant question.

An email could start with something as simple as this:

"Good Afternoon. My name is Officer John Smith with the Public Safety Department. The reason I'm writing is because I saw you present at the student leadership summit and I'm interested in having you present to my officers in the future."

Always start your written communications with the *Universal Greeting* and they will be much more effective.

Start every professional and personal interaction with the *Universal Greeting* and you will increase the likelihood of beginning on a positive note and not escalate a situation unnecessarily.

"The reason to deliver a great Universal Greeting is to create a reasonable doubt in your contact's mind that you are not a jerk."

Gary T. Klugiewicz, VDI Director of Training

Perspective Taking – Interlude

Empathy can be difficult. In our live training, we often show a video of a college-classroom situation where the end point is a woman being taken to the ground and handcuffed. Then, we ask half the students to take the perspective of the individuals of authority (college teacher and law enforcement professionals) and the other half to take the perspective of the woman (student in class). Next, we ask each side to share their assigned perspective with the whole class.

As you can imagine, it is often difficult for those whose profession is teaching or law enforcement (individuals of authority) to take the perspective of the woman — and for non-law-enforcement individuals in class to take the perspective of the individuals of authority. In fact, it is quite difficult.

You have already learned the Core Principle of Vistelar's conflict management methodology (treat people with dignity by showing respect) and the Empathy Triad (acknowledge their perspective, seek to understand, anticipate their needs), which should always be applied to your interactions with people, even if you disagree with them.

As a law enforcement professional, there are times when you need to extend these principles further and apply them even if you do not respect the other person's behavior.

You might view a person as a hardened criminal but, to be effective at conflict management and have the best chance for a positive outcome, you must treat him or her with dignity and work hard to take his or her perspective.

As stated earlier, dignity is an inalienable right of all human beings so your opinion of other's behavior should have no effect on your ability to take their perspective (practice Empathy) and treat them with dignity.

6a. Listening Introduction

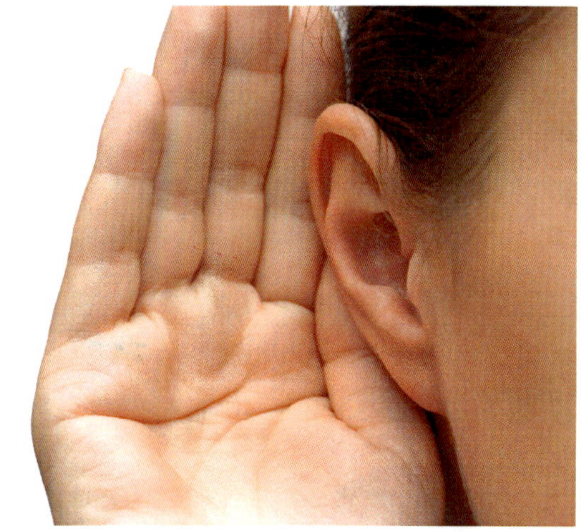

Empathy is a professional approach for communicating concern and gathering information about another person: active intelligent gathering. It is the engine that drives the effectiveness of all Vistelar customer service and conflict management and non-escalation tactics.

The *Universal Greeting* begins this process, and following the relevant-question step, it continues with the *Beyond Active Listening* tactic.

Whether you are interacting with a student, campus staff member, colleague, friend or family member, your level of *Empathy* for the other person will determine your success.

Empathy is a challenge when you first meet a person because you know little about him or her, which makes taking that person's perspective difficult. However, you can still apply the first element of the *Empathy Triad*: acknowledge their perspective. Whatever the other person might say, you can respond with statements like: "Thank you for sharing that with me." — "Hmm, I never thought of it that way." — "Huh, that's interesting."

Once you have gathered additional information about the other person, you can apply the second two elements of the *Empathy Triad*:

1. Seek to understand the other person. Try to understand his or her perspective so you can treat the individual the way you would want to be treated if you were that person and in the exact same circumstances. The better you can understand the other person's perspective, the more effective you will be with customer service and conflict management.

2. Anticipate the other person's needs. Consider what that person will be thinking or feeling immediately following the interaction, the next day or later. The goal is to treat the other person the way that person may not even know he or she wants to be treated.

The *Beyond Active Listening* tactic begins with applying the following *Active Listening* techniques.

- Focus all of your attention on the other person. Do not check your watch, phone or the clock.
- Keep arms and legs uncrossed. Do not fidget.
- Put on the appropriate facial expression for the situation
- Maintain appropriate eye contact
- Nod, and if appropriate, take notes to acknowledge points made
- Make brief comments like: "Tell me what is going on" — "Talk to me a bit" — "Go On" — "Really?" — "I see" — "Tell me more" — "And then what happened?"
- Listen with all your senses. Besides just hearing the other person's words and tone of voice, be attentive to visual cues like facial expression, eye contact, posture, and body language; how he or she smells, been drinking?; via touch, the person's level of tenseness; and even how the air might taste, smoker?
- Let the other person finish a complete thought before responding

The goal of *Active Listening* is for the other person to feel: a) he or she has been heard and understood, and b) you are interested in what he or she is trying to communicate.

"One of the most sincere forms of respect is actually listening to what another has to say."
Bryant H. McGill, author, Nobel Prize nominee (1969 to present)

To be effective at customer service and conflict management, you should listen more than you talk; that is why we have two ears and one mouth. When other people are talking, you should be listening.

What usually happens instead? When the other person is talking, you are probably thinking about what you are going to say next. Far too often, people are so busy formulating a response they do not hear a word of what the other person is saying.

"Listen with the intent to understand, not the intent to reply."
Stephen Covey, *The 7 Habits of Highly Effective People* (1932 - 2012)

Listen to understand and learn. Your brain will have plenty of time to figure out what to say next after the other person has finished talking.

6b. Beyond Active Listening

The *Beyond Active Listening* tactic enables you to gather more information about a person (active intelligence gathering) than what you might learn through just *Active Listening*, with the goal of increasing your effectiveness at customer service, conflict management and threat assessment.

You must realize that people frequently do not say what they mean, especially in conflict situations. Their words are often smoke screens to mask what they are really thinking and feeling. That is why *Active Listening* is rarely sufficient. You must dig deeper by going *Beyond Active Listening.*

> *"If you are only listening with your ears, you are not hearing everything"*
>
> Dave Young, Arma Director of Training

If you do, you will be amazed what you can learn about the needs, wants and desires of another person, which you can then use to be more effective at preventing and managing conflict and delivering exceptional customer service.

PEOPLE OFTEN DON'T SAY WHAT THEY MEAN

THEREFORE, WE MUST:

LISTEN ACTIVELY

DIG DEEPER BY LISTENING WITH ALL YOUR SENSES

GO BEYOND ACTIVELY LISTENING

There are six elements of the *Beyond Active Listening* tactic:

1. **Clarify** — Ask questions with the goal of learning more about the other person; however, so you don't come across as an interrogator, ask permission ("I've got some questions to ask – is that OK?" or "May I ask some clarifying questions so I better understand?") and ask open-ended and opinion-seeking questions.
2. **Paraphrase** — If you feel the need to interject yourself into the conversation in order to gain a better understanding about what a person is saying, start with "Let me see if I understand what you are saying." Then, repeat in your words what you believe is the meaning behind the other person's words – and ask if you are correct.

   "Let me see if I understand what you are saying. "You are saying [and then share your interpretation of his or her words]. Do I have this right?"

   In addition to the "You are saying ..." phrase, you can use other phrases, such as: "You are thinking ..." — "It is your point of view ..." — "It seems to you ... " — "In your experience ..." — "As you see it ..."

This element helps you gather additional information about the other person and reduces the likelihood of misunderstandings. Be sure to always end this tactic with a confirming question.

Note: if the other person is expressing strong emotions, it is often helpful to start with the *Reflect* element (see below) to acknowledge his or her feelings before using the *Paraphrase* element to express your understanding of the content of what the person is saying.

3. **Reflect** — Acknowledge the person's emotions and give him or her the opportunity to talk out his or her feelings (rather than act them out). After using your *Active Listening* skills, state your view of what the other person is feeling and why — succinctly and precisely as possible.

"Hmmm. You're feeling anxious because you're not sure where your mom is. Do I have this right?"

Keep your *Reflection* tentative and be sure to give the other person time to respond to your question.

Note that strong emotions — anger, hate, fear — usually don't need reflecting because the other person is often well aware of these feelings. Instead, use the *Reflect* element to bring out more subtle emotions that the other person might not recognize he or she is feeling.

This element helps you understand the nature and intensity of the other person's emotions. Be sure to always end this tactic with a confirming question.

4. **Mirror** — Subtly imitate the other person's subconscious body orientation, posture, mannerisms, breathing rate, eye contact, tone of voice and talking pace, but never his or her negative body language.

This element can cause the person being mirrored to feel more connected with the person exhibiting the mirrored behavior. Therefore, it helps build rapport, trust and liking so the other person is more open to communicating with you. In addition, doing this can help you gain a better understanding of the person you are mirroring.

Note: *mirroring* is different than *modeling calmness* (demonstrating the behavior you want the other person to replicate), which is covered in the *Crisis Interventions* section later in this manual.

5. **Advocate** — Acknowledge the issue and express how you and the other person should work together to address it. "That sounds like a big problem; let's work together to figure out how to fix it." or "That's unacceptable; let's both see what we can do about it."

This element communicates concern and it gets the interaction correctly focused on the problem, ratherthan on you.

BEYOND ACTIVE LISTENING

- CLARIFY
- PARAPHRASE
- REFLECT
- MIRROR
- ADVOCATE
- SUMMARIZE

6. **Summarize** — At the end of an interaction, provide a detailed summary of what was decided and/or what will happen next, followed by a question asking for confirmation; e.g., "Let me see if we both understand what we agreed to" [and then share summary]. "Is that your understanding?"

   This element ensures you and the other person are on the same page.

One More Element

If the other person is unwilling to talk, it's obviously difficult to apply the Beyond Active Listening tactic. Here is a seventh element that you can use in such situations.

7. **Prompt** — If the other person is closed-lipped, gently invite him or her to talk:
   - Ask open-ended questions ("What do you think about ..." — "I'm wondering about ...")
   - Make an observation ("Nice shoes." — "Sure is raining hard.")
   - Reflect on his or her visual cues ("You seem pleased.")
   - Ask questions to identify his or her interests ("Do you like sports?")
   - Tell a brief story about something of possible interest (e.g, the current news).

Then be purposively quiet and apply your Active Listening skills. This element helps maintain dialog, which can provide further insights as to what the other person is thinking and feeling.

Even if you struggle to put yourself in another person's shoes because you have not had his or her life experiences, using the *Beyond Active Listening* tactic can help you comprehend the person's mental and emotional response to a situation, and in turn, increase your effectiveness at conflict management and providing exceptional customer service.

"When people talk, listen completely. Most people never listen."
Ernest Hemingway, American Novelist (1899 - 1961)

Remember the primary goals of the *Beyond Active Listening* tactic:

1. For the other person to feel he or she has been heard and understood
2. For the other person to feel you are interested in what he or she is trying to communicate
3. To gather information about the other person, which will help you in managing whatever conflict that might arise, such as his or her:
   - Intentions
   - Level of confidence

- Ability to understand
- Mental and emotional state
- Mental health history
- Medications he/she is taking or should be taking
- Capabilities to deliver on a threat

People Are Listening To You

The people with whom you interact are also "listening" to you — and not just to your spoken words. Your non-verbals and paraverbals are equally, if not more, important to how people interpret your communications.

For example, in the paraphrase tactic, the words must be presented with neutrality (via a calm tone of voice and non-verbals). If not, the paraphrase will sound more like judgment than *Empathy* and will not be effective.

In addition, realize that periods of silence are a component of your communication, which you should not be afraid to use. Silence gives people an opportunity to collect their thoughts and removes pressure for their immediate response.

"The sounds of silence can never be misquoted."

Coach Bob Lindsey, Vistelar Advisor

Finally, when you are with others in addressing a conflict situation, have one person do all the talking to minimize confusion. Then, if this person is not able to engage the individual, switch roles.

Remember, people will generally not remember what you said. What will stick in their head is how you made them feel.

"The level of intensity of a person's attack is driven by how poorly you've made them feel."

Dave Young, Arma Director of Training

Listening Mistakes

When using the Beyond Active Listening tactic, it is extremely important to keep the focus on the other person. Empathy is about seeing the world through the other person's eyes; taking the other person's perspective.

However, during an interaction it is easy to communicate unintentional messages that shift the focus to you. This can:

- Derail your efforts to communicate concern and gather intelligence
- Create resentment or defensiveness
- Even cause a situation to escalate

Listening Mistakes *continued*

To prevent these negative outcomes, keep the focus on the other person by avoiding these common listening mistakes:

1. Advising – counseling the other person ("What I think you should do is …" or "Next time, why don't you just try …"), which implies that he or she is incapable of making a good decision on his or her own.
2. Complementing – trying to win the other person over with praise ("You seem like an intelligent person" or "You have so much potential"), which can sound condescending or sarcastic.
3. Querying – asking the other person the reasons for his or her behavior ("Why did you do that?" or "How did you get in this situation?"), which sounds judgmental and implies your goal is to solve the other person's problem.
4. Dismissing – downplaying the other person's concerns in an effort to reassure he or she that things are not as bad as they seem ("It could be worse" — "Think on the positive side" — "At least you didn't … " — "It's not the end of the world" — "You're a lot better off than some people"), which, though well-meaning, can be interpreted as denying the other person's feelings or even insulting.
5. Identifying – saying you "know" or "understand" the other person's situation ("I know just how you are feeling" or "The same thing happened to me once so I totally understand"), which the other person can view as dismissive ("Oh yeah, how could you possibly know?!").

All these mistakes are about you; your advice, your analysis, your opinion and your experience. Do not let the focus shift to you. Keep it on the other person, so he or she feels:

- You hear and understand what he or she is saying
- You are interested in what he or she is trying to communicate
- You are trustworthy and he or she is safe in your presence

Remember, the primary goal of the Beyond Active Listening tactic is to gather additional information about the other person (active intelligence gathering), which can only be accomplished if the other person talks. Therefore, do the following to encourage the person to open up and share his or her thoughts and feelings:

- Do not make the above listening mistakes
- Actively listen
- Apply this tactic's seven elements: clarify, paraphrase, reflect, mirror, advocate, prompt, summarize
- Use all three elements of communication: words, tone of voice and non-verbals
- Make comments like the following to maintain dialog and communicate concern:

  - "I'm glad you told me"
  - "Now I think I understand why you are upset"
  - "I hear what you are saying"
  - "No wonder you are upset, anyone would be"
  - "Don't worry, I'm here to help you"

Note: once the interaction has moved past listening, Advising (see Persuasion Sequence) and Complementing / Querying (see Closure) may be appropriate.

De-Escalation

Review and What's Next

Up until this point, non-escalation tactics have been discussed. These tactics focus on predicting and preventing conflict, and if necessary, turning a defensive atmosphere into a supportive one.

- *Treat With Dignity By Showing Respect*
- *Be Alert & Decisive; Respond, Don't React*
- *Showtime Mindset*
- *Proxemics 10-5-2*
- *Universal Greeting*
- *Beyond Active Listening*

In addition, practicing these tactics will improve your relationships with students, campus staff, colleagues, friends and family. And, if you struggle with conflict with any of these people and, as a result, avoid it or accommodate them by giving in, the use of these tactics will enhance your confidence to deal with conflict head-on, rather than shying away from it.

Next, de-escalation tactics will be discussed. These tactics focus on recovering from a conflict or crisis situation:

- *Redirections*
- *Persuasion Sequence*
- *Crisis Interventions*

The *Redirections* tactic is used when someone questions you, expresses frustration or anger, verbally abuses you, or is on a rambling tangent from what you are trying to accomplish.

The *Persuasion Sequence* is used when someone is questioning, resisting or refusing a request.

Crisis Interventions are used when someone is in crisis and displaying at-risk behaviors.

If a situation with another person has escalated to conflict or crisis, before using these de-escalation tactics, do your best to apply what you have already learned:

- Show them respect
- Take their perspective (*Empathy*)
- Don't speak reactively
- Maintain your *Emotional Equilibrium*
- Think "when then," not "if then"
- Imagine stepping onto a stage (*Showtime Mindset*)
- Respect their personal space
- Do not stand directly in front of them
- Control distance (*10-5-2*)
- Have a pre-planned escape route
- Answer their four questions (*Universal Greeting*)
- Give them an opportunity to talk and then listen with all your senses
- Acknowledge their perspective
- Communicate concern and gather information (*Beyond Active Listening*)

Notes:

- In most cases, prior to using any of the three de-escalation tactics (*Redirections*, *Persuasion Sequence*, *Crisis Interventions*), you should introduce yourself with the *Universal Greeting* and then listen to the other person's response to your "relevant question" using the *Beyond Active Listening* tactic.
- Although *Beyond Active Listening* is primarily a non-escalation tactic, it is useful in de-escalation. Encouraging another person to talk and then listening to him or her is the ultimate in showing of respect, so it can have a dramatic effect in calming a situation.
- The primary goals of the three de-escalation tactics (*Redirections*, *Persuasion Sequence*, *Crisis Interventions*) are everyone's safety and shifting the situation to a positive outcome.
- If you struggle in dealing with conflict, having the knowledge, skills and abilities to apply these three de-escalation tactics will significantly increase your confidence in addressing anger, verbal abuse, at-risk behavior and other clashes.

Framework: Conflict and Crisis

In this section you will learn Vistelar's de-escalation tactics that apply to these two elements of Vistelar's 6 C's of Conflict Management: *Point-Of-Impact Conflict Management Framework*™.

Conflict: When questioning, anger or verbal abuse enters into an interaction.

Goal: de-escalation to prevent heightened emotions from progressing to crisis or a physical altercation.

Crisis: When the person with whom you are interacting is displaying at-risk behaviors.

Primary Goal: everyone's safety.

Secondary Goal: recovery, to end the crisis.

Note that all interactions have a Context and Contact element but only some interactions progress to Conflict and/or Crisis.

As you progress through this section, consider how the de-escalation tactics you are learning apply to these two elements of an interaction.

7. Redirections

The *Redirections* tactic is used when someone questions you, expresses frustration or anger, verbally abuses you, or is on a rambling tangent from what you are trying to accomplish.

Think about what you would do if someone threw a punch at you. Would you just sit there and take the punch? Obviously not. You would try to block or deflect it. You should do the same with a verbal punch — redirect it rather than just take it, or worse, get sucked in and end up in an argument or a fight.

Here is how the *Redirections* tactic works.

When someone verbally attacks you, respond with something like, "I hear you, but… ," and then either return to what you were trying to accomplish or leave, if leaving is appropriate for the situation.

Note the attack is acknowledged, but is not addressed. The goal of the *Redirections* tactic is not to accomplish the objective of the interaction; it is just to move past the attack and either get back on point or leave.

There are two types of *Redirections*:

1. *Acknowledge* ➔ *Back To Issue*
2. *Divert Attention*

REDIRECTIONS

- ACKNOWLEDGE → BACK TO ISSUE
- DIVERT ATTENTION

With the *Acknowledge* → *Back To Issue* type, there are two parts: 1) acknowledging his or her comments with a statement like "I appreciate that," "I hear you," "I got that," "I see," and 2) getting back to the issue at hand. Your message to the other person is that:

- You have heard them
- Their attack has no impact on you
- The interaction must be focused on your agenda, not theirs

Here are some examples of the *Acknowledge* → *Back To Issue* type:

- "I hear you, however we have an issue to address; can you work with me here?"
- "I see and I'd probably feel the same way if I were in your shoes; nevertheless, you were driving twenty-five mile per hour over the speed limit and I have a job to do here."
- "I appreciate that. Other folks in the area felt the same way until they saw the facts. Let's review what we have here."
- "Whoa! Time out! Is there anything I can do to help? If not, can we get back to the issue?"
- "You might be right, but we still need to find a way to solve this problem."
- "I appreciate that you feel that way and I want to solve the problem. Can you work with me here?"
- "I get that you're upset. However, there are children present that don't need to hear that language. If you must use profanity, let's go outside while we figure this out."
- "I appreciate that you've had problems here in the past, but you haven't dealt with me before, so let's see what I can do to help."
- "You seem upset and I'm sorry you feel that way; however, can we get back to the issue at hand?"
- [If the other person is walking towards you with their hands up] "I appreciate that you're looking out for both our safety, but please put your hands down and let me know how I can help you."

The *Beyond Active Listening* elements of *Reflect* and *Paraphrase* can also be used as *Acknowledge* → *Back To Issue* type *Redirections*. For example:

- "You're feeling frustrated because it took us a long time to get here; but, we're here now so let's see if we can figure out some way to resolve this."
- "Let me see if I understand what you are saying. What you are telling me is [and then repeat in your words what you believe is the meaning behind their words]. Do I have this right?"

These two tactics are respectful and effective ways to interrupt a verbal attack. By stating what another person is feeling or saying, he or she will almost always stop talking to listen to what you have to say. Then, you can take back control of the interaction.

Sometimes, even when you have adequately explained the reason for a situation, the other person will continue to ask "Why" over and over again and a Redirection can be effective. For example:

- "Sir, I've answered your question and explained why. Can we get back on track with why I'm here?"

When acknowledging the other person's comments, be careful not to say that you "know" or "understand" the other person's situation. Such statements could prompt an angry, "You don't know how I feel! — how could you?" type of response. Instead, start the *Redirection* with statements like: "I appreciate that," "I hear you," "I got that," "I see."

Also, be careful about using humor because it can sound disrespectful. *Redirections* should not sound like a counterpunch.

Becoming Bully-Proof

In our youth anti-bullying programs, the *Redirections* tactic is one of the main tactics we teach.

The bully yells, "You are an idiot" — and the practiced response is "I hear what you said -- was there something important you need to tell me?" and the child walks away.

Redirections are like a suit of armor that make kids (and adults) bully-proof.

The *Divert Attention* type of *Redirection* has the goal of giving the other person time to calm down or to forget why he or she is upset. In addition, it gives you the opportunity to leave if you sense a safety issue and if leaving is appropriate for the situation.

Here are some examples of this type:

- "Whoops, I think I see someone coming. Oh, false alarm — OK, where were we?"
- "What was that noise?"
- "I forgot my [keys, cell phone or needed form]. Give me a few moments."
- "The *Universal Greeting* — sometimes this approach to initiating a contact is so different than what people are used to, it can stop disruptive behavior in its tracks
- "I need to take a bathroom break. I'll be right back."

We had a client who made balloon animals. He would often interrupt a rant by saying, "By the way, what type of animal would you like to be?" Then, he would pull a balloon out of his pocket and make that animal. Once he had the animal made, he would get back to the business at hand.

When using the *Redirections* tactic, be careful to preserve the other person's dignity. This tactic is not a dismissal. No matter how badly you are being treated, you are still dealing with a human being and you need to treat him or her as such. Therefore, always question if the *Redirections* tactic is appropriate or if it would be better to listen to the other person in order to gather more information using the *Beyond Active Listening* tactic.

When dealing with verbal attacks, do not take the bait, defend your ego or lash out. Instead, focus on accomplishing your goal for the interaction, or if necessary and appropriate, leave the situation.

Do not concern yourself with the other person's abusive comments. Your job is not to fix his or her attitude; it is to get back on track with the goal of the interaction.

Note: the above scripted examples of *Redirections* are provided just to get you started in developing your own scripts you can put to memory and practice with colleagues, friends and family. When faced with real-world verbal attacks, just winging it does not work. Instead, you need lots of "arrows" in your quiver that you have memorized and are comfortable and competent in using, because you have engrained them into your mental muscle memory.

Therefore, please take the time to consider the situations you commonly face, write out appropriate *Redirections* scripts and practice those scripts out loud, ensuring the appropriate words, non-verbals and paraverbals are in alignment with the situation.

"If you don't tell them what to say you shouldn't be shocked on what comes out of their mouths."

Dave Young, Arma Director of Training

Once you become proficient at the *Redirections* tactic, you might start enjoying verbal attacks for two reasons:

- You know the other person cannot get under your skin and disrupt your *Emotional Equilibrium.*
- You are confident you have the knowledge, skills and abilities to respond, in an effective manner, to whatever the other person may throw at you.

Ethical Intervention

The *Redirections* tactic can be used to "tap out" your partner or colleague (*Ethical Intervention*) when you see them taking an action they will likely regret or that will get them in trouble. Just by stepping in you "acknowledge" the situation and then you can get things back on track with an appropriate statement, such as:

- "Jim, let me ask a few questions here while you check the backyard. OK?"
- "Jim, the computer in our squad isn't working; can you check it out? I'll take over here."
- "Jim, my phone died and I need to talk with Mike regarding this. Can you go outside and call him? I will be out in a minute."

Relative to addressing verbal attacks, there is one more important point: stick to your lines. Do not partake in any negative side conversations or "trash talk," such as offhand remarks or derogatory comments that might be heard by others or caught on camera and come back to haunt you.

The Word on the Street: The Importance of Ethical Intervention

Taking the time to notice a situation going wrong and doing something to prevent it from getting it worse will always be worth it. Vistelar co-founder Gary T. Klugiewicz likes to say, "What takes more time… the extra 30 seconds it takes to talk with somebody or the use of force report?" While he often says this in the context of interacting with the public, it holds true for when interacting with other officers.

Depending on the type of day an officer is having, the nature of the call at hand, or the verbal attacks being slung their way, you never know when an officer is about to go from bad to worse. In knowing your fellow officers, going *Beyond Active Listening*, and being aware of their *Conflict Triggers*, you can act as a support and an ally to them in a way they may not even know they needed. Career-ending decisions can happen in a heartbeat. Being an officer who is willing to step in and step up for their colleagues will not only help protect their careers, but also the profession itself.

8. Persuasion Sequence

The *Persuasion Sequence* is used when someone is questioning, resisting or refusing a request. In campus safety, you will encounter numerous challenging situations- non-compliant people, people in crisis, intoxicated students, and so on. You will generally have to persuade them to change their behavior and gain compliance without the use of force. The *Persuasion Sequence* is extremely effective in working towards that objective.

The goal of the *Persuasion Sequence* is to

provide an opportunity in a respectful manner for the other person to cooperate with your request before you are faced with taking whatever further action is necessary.

"Persuasion is often more effectual than force."

Aesop, Ancient Greek story teller
(620 - 564 BCE)

This tactic is almost always used following a four-step Universal Greeting, such as with a person driving over the speed limit:

"Good morning.
I'm Officer Jones with the campus police.
The reason I stopped you is because my radar showed you were going 55 in a 35 mile per hour zone.
Is there any reason why you were driving so fast?"

Once the driver answers, you might ask him or her to provide a driver's license and car registration. If he or she questions, resists or refuses your request, you would use the Persuasion Sequence to try to get cooperation. In using this tactic, you should only progress to the next step if the previous step did not gain cooperation.

Here are the three steps of this tactic:

1. Explain why, confirm understanding

To prevent people from imagining their own reasons as to why you are asking them to do something, which can become a roadblock for cooperation: a) provide a reason for your request (usually due to a law, policy, rule or prior agreement), b) give them a rationale for the reason, and c) confirm their understanding of the reason.

"The reason for my request is that the law states that anyone operating a motor vehicle must surrender their driver's license to any law enforcement officer, when requested, to confirm they are legally able and licensed to operate the motor vehicle. Do you understand?"

Then end this step by asking again for their cooperation. If they again, question, resist or refuse your request, you would progress to step #2.

2. Offer options, let them choose — a) present positive option(s); b) present negative or less-positive option(s); c) emphasize the positive option(s).

Do this using this script:
"We have some good options here" — and then:

a. Present a vivid description of the positive option(s)

b. Present a vivid description of the negative or less-positive option(s)

c. Put a final emphasis on the positive

PERSUASION SEQUENCE

- **EXPLAIN WHY, CONFIRM UNDERSTANDING**
- **OFFER OPTIONS, LET THEM CHOOSE**
- **GIVE OPPORTUNITY TO RECONSIDER**

Here is a generic example:

> "We have some good options here. If you cooperate, we can [and then share a positive option]. However, if you refuse, we will [and then share a negative or less-positive option]. It's your choice but can you work with me here?"

Here is an example specific to campus public safety:

> "We have some good options here. If you cooperate, you'll get home tonight, get your homework done and sleep in your own bed. However, if you refuse, I am required to arrest you, call your parents and tow your vehicle – and then you'll spend tonight in jail. By the time you get home it will cost you more than $800 in bail and towing fees. It's your choice but can you work with me here?"

If you have effectively practiced *Empathy*, you should be able to see the world through the other person's eyes, and make the positive option sound quite good and the negative or less-positive option sound much less attractive. In describing the two options, be as specific as possible and paint a vivid picture.

Then make it clear the choice is theirs, not yours, which takes all the pressure off of you and puts it on them. It is their decision as to what will happen next and they are empowered to make that choice.

"You have options. I don't have any options. I have a duty to perform."

Gary T. Klugiewicz, VDI Director of Training

By offering options to a person who is questioning, resisting or refusing a request, you are providing him or her with the opportunity to save face while agreeing to cooperate.

Always end this step by asking again for their cooperation. If they again, question, resist or refuse your request, you would progress to step #3.

3. Give opportunity to reconsider

If this final step of the *Persuasion Sequence* is needed, you would a) ask them to reconsider, and b) express a hope that he or she would do so.

For example:

- "You seem like a reasonable person. Would you please reconsider?"
- "Is there anything I can say to help you change your mind?"
- "I know we both want the safest solution possible. Would you please reconsider your decision?"

And then follow with a statement like, "I would hope so."

If the other person has not cooperated after this third step, your options here will vary depending on the situation. What is important is that you know your options and have a preplanned response to the situations you will likely face (see *Take Appropriate Action*).

Please Note ...

Even though "ask and explain why" is one of the five approaches to showing respect, there are times, such as the existence of a safety issue with immediate compliance required, when you must tell someone to do something rather than ask them. In such situations, issue a short, direct command.

At any time during *Persuasion Sequence*, you may need to use other tactics, such as *Beyond Active Listening* to hear them out or *Redirections* to address verbal abuse, so you can get back on track before continuing with the sequence.

When using the *Persuasion Sequence*, it is important each step is used without excessive repetition. You do not want to get into a cycle of providing exhaustive explanations, offering numerous options or giving multiple opportunities to reconsider. Instead, just move deliberately through each step, with the goal of providing an opportunity for the other person to cooperate before you are faced with taking whatever further action is necessary.

Think about the number of times someone, whether it is a student, campus staff member, a colleague, a family member or a friend, questions, resists or refuses a request.

"Why do I need to do that?" — "I'm not getting out of my car" — "I'm not giving that back" — "I'm not leaving" — "I'm going to miss that deadline" — "I can't give your money back" — "I won't be coming in on the weekend" — "I don't want to do my homework" — "I'm not going to bed."

Not everyone deals with verbal attacks or crisis on a regular basis, but no one can escape the daily experience of having people question, resist or refuse requests. That is why the *Persuasion Sequence* is the most used of the three de-escalation tactics.

9. Crisis Interventions

Introduction

Crisis Interventions are used when someone is in crisis and displaying at-risk behaviors.

A crisis occurs when an individual has an experience that exceeds his or her coping skills, which can happen to anyone. However, there are issues that can contribute to the frequency and severity of crisis, which can be classified as:

1. Long-term issues, such as psychiatric disorder, cognitive disability, addiction, or history of trauma
2. Under the influence issues, such as being actively affected by alcohol or drugs
3. Short-term issues, such as failing grades, financial loss, violence, sexual assault, or relationship loss (death, divorce, abandonment), incarceration or financial loss.

Crisis often leads to a range of at-risk behaviors that can cause emotional or physical harm to the individual in crisis or to others. Therefore, it is important you know how to identify the various states of crisis and how to respond correctly to a crisis situation.

Generally, people in crisis do not act out because of the issues identified above (long term, under the influence, short term). Instead, their behaviors are due to over-stimulation, an urgent need, or both. These behaviors present along a continuum of states that can be classified as baseline, stress, acute and recovery.

- Baseline: behaviors typical for an individual's:
  - Natural Personality — shy, grumpy, outgoing, happy
  - Background — cultural upbringing, social development, history of trauma
  - Mental Health — cognitive disabilities, psychiatric disorders
  - Physical Health — chronic pain, diabetes, heart disease
- Stress: heightened anxiety, with these possible responses:
  - Physical: tremors, headache, rapid breathing, increased perspiration, fatigue
  - Emotional: anger, panic, irritability, hopelessness, inappropriate emotions
  - Behavioral: fidgeting, pacing, clenched fist, boxer stance, crowding, resisting
  - Verbal: yelling, name calling, cursing, mumbling, blaming, interrupting, ignoring
  - Nonverbal: inappropriate expressions, staring, target glancing, refusing eye contact
  - Atypical: body rocking, hand flapping, shutting down, lashing out, repeating,
- Acute: unbearable anxiety, with these possible responses:
  - Loss of cognitive, emotional and/or behavioral control
  - Urgent need to end the emotional pain or stop the real or perceived threat
  - Direct threats to harm themselves or others
  - Physical violence against themselves or others

    Note: individuals with cognitive disabilities often stay in the acute state of crisis for long periods of time.
- Recovery: continued anxiety, but in process of returning to pre-crisis level of functioning with these possible behavioral responses:
  - Emotional: embarrassment, regret, rationalizing, apologetic
  - Behavioral: crying, calm, withdrawn, unresponsive, in denial, tired

  Note: individuals in the recovery state of crisis are at risk of returning to acute state.

Trauma Informed Care

If you are required to get involved in a crisis situation, it is important to understand the principles of Trauma Informed Care (TIC).

TIC is an approach to interacting with others that acknowledges the effects of psychological, emotional and physical trauma on people's behavior and considers these effects in how interactions are handled. TIC asks "What happened to you?" rather than "What is wrong with you."

Trauma can be classified as:

- Acute trauma: A single event — experienced or witnessed — of grave physical or emotional threat or harm, such as serious accident or illness, homicide, suicide, physical or sexual assault, military trauma, terrorism, natural disaster, or abrupt separation from a loved one through death, abandonment, incarceration, or other circumstance.
- Complex trauma: Prolonged exposure to traumatic experiences, such as neglect, maltreatment, domestic violence, substance abuse, mental illness, chronic illness, bullying, homelessness, poverty or war.
- Historical trauma: Cumulative wounding transmitted across generations within an ethnic or racial minority.
- Sanctuary trauma: Overt or covert traumatic experiences within mental health, educational, foster care, religious and other institutions.
- Secondary trauma: Learning about another person's trauma.

A history of trauma can lead to a vulnerability for re-traumatization — an action or situation that is a reminder of a traumatic event. Such a reminder can rapidly push a person from his or her baseline behavior state to a stress or even acute state of a crisis.

A "trauma informed" approach to interactions acknowledges this reality and emphasizes:

- The use of active intelligence gathering about an individual's trauma history in order to minimize the possibility of re-traumatization. Active intelligence gathering can be accomplished by debriefing with others who know the person, using the Beyond Active Listening tactic, and reviewing the person's medical history if available.
- The need to avoid reminding the individual of a traumatic event by not:
  - Blaming, shaming or labeling
  - Asking about the individual's trauma or forcing him or her to talk about it
  - Yelling or becoming angry when the individual acts out
  - Touching without permission and direction from a mental health professional, unless required by an emergency situation
  - Exposing the individual to people or situations that may serve as a reminder of the trauma event. Possible reminders include persons in uniform, superior or authoritarian attitudes, former tormentors or attackers, conversation, behavior, or media involving violence or sexual situations, and kissing or other public displays of affection by others.

Initial Goal: Everyone's Safety

The initial goal is any crisis situation is everyone's safety until the situation is stabilized, so make that your focus. Realize that the acute stage of crisis can happen quickly, with a response of physical violence.

When faced with an individual in crisis do not address the situation alone, unless there is no other option. Seek someone else to assist you, preferably a mental health professional. In addition, always be ready to call for backup.

Also, when approaching a person in crisis, be aware that some might be delusional, under the influence of drugs or alcohol, or have cognitive limitations due to dementia, Alzheimer's, a brain injury, or autism. Therefore, take these steps to keep everyone safe (originated by Jane Dresser, RN - Director, Medical-Psychiatric Nursing Consultants, Inc.):

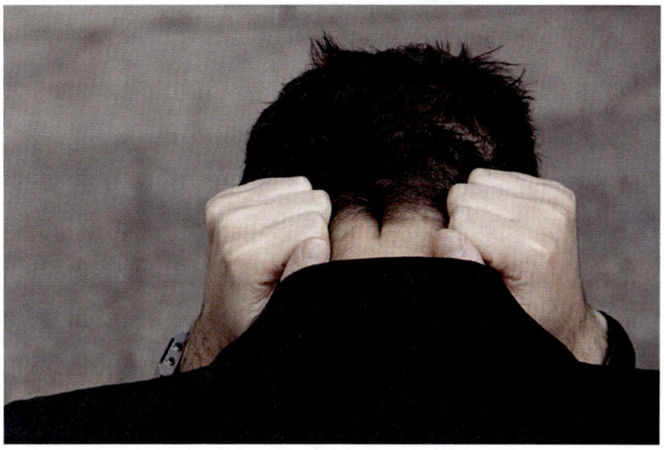

1. Attempt to get their attention. Slowly move into their line of sight, ask politely for them to look at you, and slowly wave your hands.
2. Check their perception of reality — "Where are you?" — What time/day is it?" — "What are you hearing?" — "What do you see?"
3. Attempt to establish rapport and safety — "Mary, I'm here to help you" — "It's okay, you're safe with me."
4. Explain your perception of reality — "Sam, you are in the student union" — "I can't hear what you are thinking" — "I don't see bugs, but come over here with me where it's safe" Note, you are not denying their reality; you are simply sharing yours.
5. Move towards resolution — "Alice, let's get you home. Who should I call?" — "Bill, tell me what you need right now, so I can help." — "OK, here is exactly what we are going to do …"

Promoting Recovery

Beyond safety, a secondary goal in a crisis situation is Recovery, a return of the individual to his or her pre-crisis level of functioning. The crisis intervention tactics presented below address this goal.

Many of the conflict management tactics presented earlier can assist with the goal of Recovery, such as:

- *Showtime Mindset*
- *Proxemics 10-5-2*
- *Universal Greeting*
- *Beyond Active Listening*
- *Redirections*
- *Persuasion Sequence*

These non-escalation and de-escalation tactics are invaluable during the baseline, stress, and recovery stages of crisis to prevent escalation to the acute stage. However, they may be less effective because they rely on rational thinking. Individuals in the acute stage of crisis typically lose cognitive and emotional control and may respond poorly, if at all, to questions, redirections or persuasion.

In these situations, there are additional strategies to use. As stated above, at-risk behaviors by an individual in crisis are generally due to over-stimulation, an urgent unmet need or both, which can be addressed via the use of these approaches (originated by Joel Lashley, Vistelar advisor and author of *Confidence In Conflict For Healthcare Professionals*).

CRISIS MANAGEMENT

- REDUCE STIMULATION
- SEPARATE AND SUPPORT
- ADAPT COMMUNICATION
- MEET URGENT UNMET NEEDS

1. **Reduce Stimulation:** less is better, as long as safety isn't compromised.
   - Manage proxemics: distance, relative positioning and hand placement — don't crowd, step back, stand at an angle, move slowly, keep hands in sight
   - Turn down the noise—soften your voice volume and tone; turn off/down televisions, radios, sirens, alarms, etc.
   - Soften the lights—turn them down if doing so doesn't compromise safety
2. **Separate and Support:** provide for the individual's privacy as much as possible.
   - Take him or her to an area out of public view and, if that is not possible, dismiss onlookers. Keep enough trained staff on scene for safety, but out of site when feasible
   - Provide support by calling in trained professionals, interpreters, and staff who have previously
   - Model calmness by demonstrating the behavior you want the other person to replicate.
     - Practice reverse yelling—the quieter you get the quieter they will eventually get
     - Speak slowly if they are speaking fast
     - Breathe calmly and deeply if they are hyperventilating
     - Display the appropriate non-verbals – if you want them to be concerned, look concerned; if you want them to be unafraid, look confident

   Note: all behavior equalizes – people will match your behavior if it is appropriate and consistent. Telling or asking people to calm down does not work, but you can lead them down by modeling the behavior you are seeking.
3. **Adapt Communication:**
   - Slow the interaction down
   - Use a "one voice" approach where only a single person talks to the individual. One voice = communication; two voices = noise; three or more voices = chaos
   - Wear the appropriate expression — show confidence, concern, empathy
   - Frequently use the individual's name to build an emotional connection

- and help the other person follow the conversation and stay engaged
- Give only one direction or ask only one question at a time
- Use five or less simple words per sentence to make it easier for the individual to process your comments
- Pause frequently and offer up to 20 seconds of silence before repeating yourself, to ensure the individual has the needed time to process your comments
- Make a safety statement like: "You're safe with me; let me help"
- State the obvious, such as: "You were in a car accident"

4. **Meet Urgent Unmet Needs:**

   People in crisis cannot begin recovery if they have an urgent need that is not being addressed. Offering water, food, toileting, privacy, a blanket, a phone call, or whatever else a person in crisis might not be able to ask for on his or her own will often quickly normalize behaviors and is a showing of respect — one of the most important human needs.

Relative to touching a person in crisis, the general rule is that you should not do so, unless an emergency situation requires it to keep the individual or others safe.

Remember, the primary goal in a crisis situation is everyone's safety until the situation is stabilized. Recovery, a return of the individual to his or her pre-crisis level of functioning, should be considered a secondary goal.

Ethical Intervention

In the heat of the moment, your partner or colleague could lose the ability to cope with a situation. This would require you to execute an Ethical Intervention, which could be as simple as saying: "Knock it off," or "I'm going to write this up as I see it." Remember that, as a contact professional, your job is to keep everyone safe — verbally if you can, physically if you must.

Important Note

The Less Than, Greater Than, Equal To concept also applies to proxemics as it relates to designing and controlling your space. For example, when interviewing a victim of trauma, it is possible to rearrange an interview room to "feel" more "equal to," which will help the victim feel more at ease in the room. Window placement, wall decorations, table positioning, and noise in the room can all effect the feel. Conversely, less windows, darker colors, tables (barriers), and loud noise (from your duty radio for example) will make the room feel intimidating (greater than) and potentially threatening.

Ending an Interaction

Review and What's Next

Up until this point, you have learned the following customer service and conflict management tactics:

- Non-escalation tactics, for predicting and preventing conflict, and if necessary, turning a defensive atmosphere into a supportive one.
  - *Treat People With Dignity By Showing Respect*
  - *Be Alert & Decisive; Respond, Don't React*
  - *Showtime Mindset*
  - *Proxemics 10-5-2*
  - *Universal Greeting*
  - *Beyond Active Listening*
- De-escalation tactics, focused on recovering from a conflict or crisis situation:
  - *Redirections*
  - *Persuasion Sequence*
  - *Crisis Interventions*

The primary goals of these three de-escalation tactics are everyone's safety, and shifting the situation to a positive outcome.

If you struggle in dealing with conflict, having the knowledge, skills and abilities to apply these three de-escalation tactics will significantly increase your confidence in addressing anger, verbal abuse, at-risk behavior and other clashes.

Next, tactics related to ending an interaction will be discussed:

- *Take Appropriate Action*
- *Closure*

The *Take Appropriate Action* tactic is used when the *Persuasion Sequence* has ended without cooperation or there is a clearly articulable safety concern.

The *Closure* tactic is used at the end of an interaction to achieve the best possible outcome and establish a strong foundation for the next interaction.

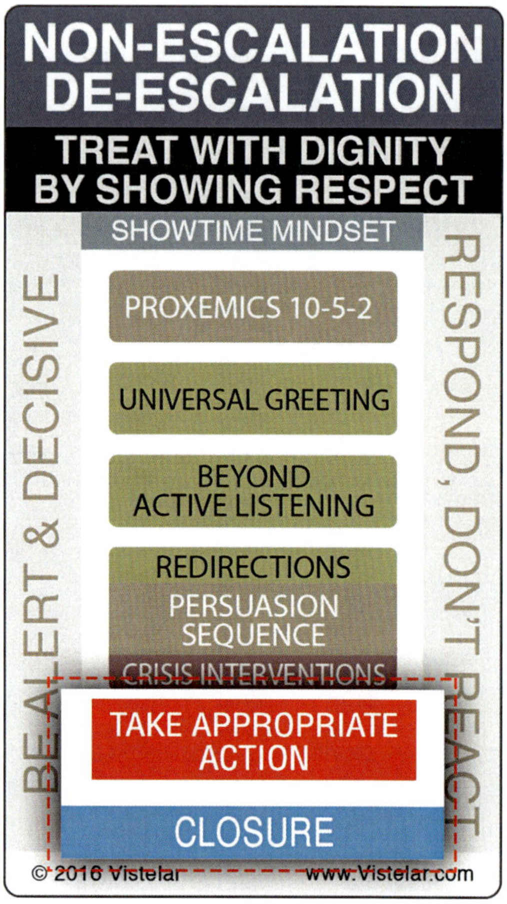

Framework: Combat and Closure

In this section you will learn Vistelar's ending-an-interaction tactics that apply to these two elements of Vistelar's 6 C's of Conflict Management: *Point-Of-Impact Conflict Management Framework*™.

Combat: When resistance or aggression results in physical engagement initiated by either party.

Goal: physical safety

Closure: Follow-through considerations, such as ensuring situation is stabilized, summarizing decisions, and reviewing the interaction.

Primary Goal: achieve best possible outcome

Secondary Goal: establish positive foundation for any future interactions

Note that only a few interactions progress to Combat, but all interactions have a Closure element.

As you progress through this section, consider how the ending-an-interactions tactics you are learning apply to these two elements of an interaction.

10. Take Appropriate Action

TAKE APPROPRIATE ACTION

- PERSUASION SEQUENCE ENDS WITHOUT COOPERATION

- CLEARLY ARTICULABLE SAFETY CONCERN

Despite best efforts, non-escalation and de-escalation do not always work:

- *Persuasion Sequence* can end without cooperation or be clearly inappropriate.

  There can be many reasons this can occur. Even if you correctly used all the non-escalation/de-escalation tactics taught in this manual, other factors affecting people's behavior may have a stronger influence. For example, they may be intoxicated, mentally ill or undergoing a medication reaction. Or they may choose not to cooperate just because they do not like the consequences of cooperation.

- A clearly articulable safety concern can occur that justifies taking action based on the totality of the circumstances known to you at the time.

When either of these criterion is met, the *Take Appropriate Action* tactic should be used, which includes these two steps:

- Know your options for taking action: be familiar with your department's policies and procedures and be prepared to operate within them.
- Have a preplanned response to situations you will likely face ("when-then thinking")

Your options for *Taking Appropriate Action* will vary according to your role within your organization, the environment you are in, the established policies and procedures, defined rules of engagement and your training and experience.

Here are some possibilities that can be used alone or in combination:

- Monitoring the situation until help arrives
- Escorting or transporting the person to another location
- Control alternatives
  - Escort holds
  - Compliance holds
  - OC spray
  - Electronic control devices
  - Decentralization techniques
- Protective alternatives
  - Vertical stuns
  - Focused strikes
  - Incapacitating techniques
  - Intermediate weapons
- Deadly force

What is extremely important is that, in both your professional and personal lives, you have a planned response to what you will do when it is necessary to *Take Appropriate Action*.

"Although rules of engagement may differ, tactics remain constant at the same level of escalation based on application and environment."

Gary T. Klugiewicz, VDI Director of Training

Ethical Intervention - Interlude

Ethical Interventions were previously mentioned in this manual within the sections covering these tactics:

- Be Alert & Decisive, Respond, Don't React
- Redirection
- Crisis Interventions

Again, the goal of an *Ethical Intervention* is to prevent or stop an incident when you believe a partner or colleague is about to take an action that he or she will likely regret or that will him or her in trouble (e.g., setting off *Conflict Triggers* of others, acting out due to anger, excessive or unnecessary use of force).

This topic is being covered again here because it is an application of *Take Appropriate Action* – the tenth element on the Non-Escalation / De-Escalation graphic.

An *Ethical Intervention*: requires you remain alert, be decisive and have a preplanned, practiced response in mind. Early intervention is the key.

"Ethics are more values in action."

Jack Hoban, author of *The Ethical Protector – Police Ethics, Tactics and Techniques* and Subject Matter Expert for the U.S. Marine Corps.

Jack's point with this quote is that it is moral to know a situation is inappropriate, but it is ethical to take action on that knowledge.

The distinction between morals and ethics can be explained by Jack's playground example. Most people know that the bullying of a child is wrong (they have strong morals in respect to bullying). Less people are willing to take action to protect the bullied child (to demonstrate ethical behavior).

As campus public safety professionals, when we see inappropriate behavior we must be ethical (by doing an *Ethical Intervention*), not just moral. There are no innocent professional bystanders.

Your ability to intervene hinges on:

- Whether or not you feel a responsibility to act (your morals)
- Whether or not you feel you are capable of acting (your ethics)

There are three types of *Ethical Interventions*:

1. Pre-Incident Prevention — This begins with your *ethical presence* (what people expect of you based on your past behavior). Then the specific tactic is a verbal intervention implemented before the point of no return.

   Saying, for example, "It's Showtime — "knock it off" — "I'm going to write this up exactly how I see it."

Ethical Intervention - Interlude *continued*

2. Direct-Contact Override — stepping in to take over the interaction, using the appropriate level of override for the situation.

   - Level 1: Verbal — e.g., "Jim, let me ask a few questions here while you check out the backyard."

   - Level 2: Positioning — getting between your partner and the subject and, if necessary, moving your partner out of the way

   - Level 3: Physical — physically removing your partner from the scene

3. Delayed Post-Incident Remedies — if an incident occurs, doing the right thing following the incident (e.g., apologize where appropriate, debrief incident to improve future performance, notify supervisor, write up the incident).

   For example, being willing to write up an incident that went wrong.

As a contact professional, your job is to keep everyone safe: verbally if you can, physically if you must. If you ignore a partner's or colleague's inappropriate actions, you are condoning them.

Before reading on, take a few minutes to consider your own experiences with the inappropriate behavior of a partner or colleague. Were you ethical in your response or just moral? Do you have a social contract with your partner as to how each of you is expected to behave in such situations?

Here is what one of our students said to his partner to establish a social contract:

> *"I am the most loyal partner you will ever have. I've got your back. I do not owe you nor will I give you my career, my marriage or family, my house or, most certainly, my freedom. Don't ever put me in a position where I may have to risk those for you and I guaranty you I will never put you in a position where you may have to risk them for me."*
>
> Rob Shiller, Detective with Denver Colorado Police Department

Combat Is A Possibility

In law enforcement and campus safety, we know that while force is rarely used to achieve a lawful objective, it is always a possibility. Dealing with resistance and non-compliance are commonplace, and defusing conflict through conversation may not always be possible. As you know, resistance can quickly turn into aggression, and when dealing with conflict, "combat" can happen in an instant.

As stated earlier, Vistelar's training focuses on addressing the entire spectrum of human conflict at the point of impact — from before an interaction begins through to the consequences of how an interaction is managed. In other words, our training is a system of non-escalation and de-escalation coupled with physical alternatives.

Combat Is A Possibility *continued*

This manual is only focused on non-escalation and de-escalation. Our physical alternative training is provided via other courses, including;

- P.O.S.C.® 1 & 2 — Principles of Subject Control
- Non-Lethal Weapons
- Lethal Weapons
- Over 50 additional specialized courses

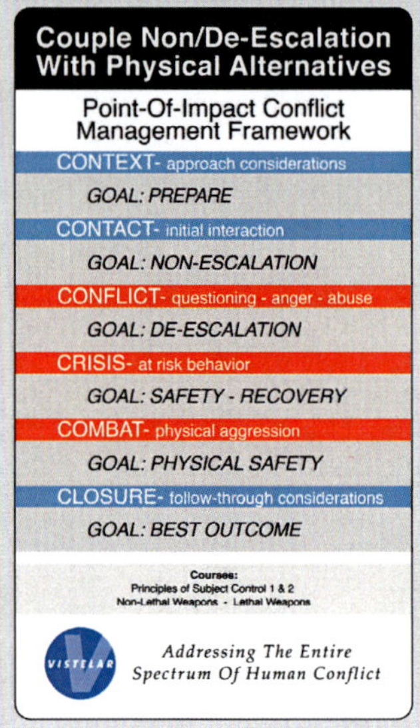

11. Closure

The *Closure* element of Vistelar's *Point-Of-Impact Conflict Management Framework*™ (6 C's of Conflict Management) includes all follow-through considerations, such as ensuring the situation is stabilized, summarizing decisions, and reviewing the interaction. The two goals of *Closure* are to:

1. Achieve the best possible outcome; in a conflict situation, end the interaction in a better place than where it started
2. Establish a positive foundation for any future interactions
   To meet these goals, you should try to end all interactions with a positive *Closure*. Realize you can do everything well up to this point, and if the *Closure* step is handled incorrectly, a negative outcome can result.

"Remember the law of primacy and law of recency — because people usually remember the beginning and end of an incident while the middle gets muddled."

Gary T. Klugiewicz, VDI Director of Training

For a routine interaction, such as with a car stop with no conflict or crisis, *Closure* can be as simple as offering a genuine thank you. However, it is best to not use a scripted response or catchphrase, such as "Have a nice day" or "No problem," which can sometimes result in a student complaint.

Instead, treat people as individuals by providing a personalized *Closure* statement. Rather than treating people as another number, treat them as human beings.

If you have practiced *Empathy* (active intelligence gathering) during the interaction, you will have plenty to work with. Identify something unique to the other person on which to comment.

Note that not using a scripted response or catchphrase is even more important in situations with conflict or crisis.

At the end of more complex interactions – especially if there was conflict or crisis – follow these steps:

- If the interaction required use of de-escalation tactics or *Combat*, ensure the situation is stable (verbal attacks stopped; recovery from crisis, appropriate action taken; everyone is safe), an initial medical assessment is performed, and if appropriate, the necessary medical care is provided. More specifically:
  1. Check their emotional level
     - Give them affirmations that they are safe and will be OK
  2. Evaluate their levels of responsiveness and alertness
     - Carefully observe
     - Ask them questions like, "What is the day of the week?" - "What time is it?" - "What color are your shoes?"
  3. Verify any physical injuries
     - Blood, bruising, broken bones
     - Trouble breathing
- Use the *Summarize* element from *Beyond Active Listening*, where you review what was decided and ask for confirmation – "Let me see if we both understand what we agreed to" [and then share detailed summary]. "Is that your understanding?" Summarizing ensures everyone is on the same page and there are no misunderstandings.
- If an interaction has gone badly, set a positive foundation for any follow-on interaction by expressing your hope for a better next encounter and by not doing anything that would poison another contact, such as using sarcasm or parting shots.
- Here are some examples of possible Closure statements for various situations:

  At the end of a routine interaction:

  - "If you have no additional questions for me, please take your time while pulling back into traffic."

  At the end of an interaction involving conflict or crisis:

  - "I'm sorry we didn't meet under better circumstances, but I'm glad we were able to work through this matter. You have my contact information; please contact me with any additional questions."

  At the end of an interaction involving an accident:

  - To check feelings of security:

    "You are safe now — it's over; let us take care of you — we are here to help."
  - To check mental alertness:

    "What is your name? — do you know where you are? — do you know what day it is?"
  - To check for any physical injuries:

    "Do you hurt anywhere? — does it hurt when you breathe? — can you wiggle your fingers/toes?"

Following an interaction, you should reflect on the interaction, either on your own or with another person, with the sole goal of improving future performance. This can be done verbally or in writing, via an incident report or other such documentation.

If a group debriefing is needed, follow these steps during the discussion:

- Initial wellness check
- How is everyone?
- What went well?
- What was learned? (if you could it again, is there anything you would do differently?)

During the debriefing everyone should try to see the situation through the eyes of both parties in the interaction. If each participant practices *Empathy*, you will be amazed as to what the group will learn to improve future performance.

If the incident requires it, you should capture the debriefing on paper. A good written incident report, especially if your actions matched the training you received, is a powerful defense if anyone questions what happened in a specific incident.

"Remember, if you don't write it down and it would make you look good, it didn't happen."

Gary T. Klugiewicz, VDI Director of Training

Note: if you always follow the tactics taught in this manual, it will be much easier to write a complete and accurate incident report because you will know exactly what you did and the order you did it. You will also be much more equipped to justify your actions because you will be able to articulate exactly what you did (and said) when you were legally justified to do so.

Finally, take care of yourself. Effective conflict management is hard work, stressful and can wear you down. As a campus public safety professional, you are likely sensitive, caring and compassionate and probably chose your career to make a difference in some way. As a result, dealing with conflict, especially if it includes verbal and/or physical abuse, can be challenging.

Many of the tactics covered in this manual are meant to help with this challenge, such as:

- Treating people with dignity by showing respect, which does not mean you need to agree with the other person
- Practicing *Empathy* rather than sharing another person's distress (feeling sympathy)
- Knowing your conflict triggers and developing guards against them
- Scripting and practicing professional responses

GOALS OF CLOSURE

- ACHIEVE BEST POSSIBLE OUTCOME

- ESTABLISH POSITIVE FOUNDATION FOR FUTURE INTERACTIONS

- Having a *Showtime Mindset*
- Using *Proxemics 10-5-2* to enhance physical safety
- Knowing how to start any interaction (*Universal Greeting*)
- Using *Redirections* instead of just taking verbal abuse
- Offering options (*Persuasion Sequence*) to make it the other person's choice as to what will happen next, instead of yours
- Knowing how to respond to a crisis situation
- Having the confidence to take appropriate action if word-based tactics fail
- Using a post-incident debriefing process that is supportive instead of critical
- Knowing you can only control the process, not the outcomes

However, despite all this, you may still experience "burnout" or other emotional trauma. If that occurs, find someone to talk with or seek counseling.

A Word About Compassion Fatigue and First Responders

Compassion fatigue, also referred to as secondary traumatic stress (STS), is common amongst professional first responders and is a condition characterized by a gradual lessening of compassion over time as a result of the constant exposure to high stress incidents, tragedy, and trauma.

Compassion fatigue can cause apathy and burnout, both of which can be detrimental to your career. Watch for the symptoms of compassion fatigue (such as increased anxiety, depression, negative attitude, loss of interest in hobbies, nightmares or sleeplessness), and work to develop a well-rounded personal self-care routine. If you are a supervisor, watch for these symptoms in your personnel and know the policies and resources your department has in place to assist them.

The graphics displayed here are available from Vistelar as wallet-sized cards. These cards provide a helpful reminder of our tactics, but they can also be used:

- During a citizen complaint debriefing. You could pull out the "Non-Escalation De-Escalation" card (often nick-named the "get out of trouble" card) and walk through the card to explain exactly the steps you took during the interaction.
- If you are asked if you have had de-escalation training during a court testimony. You could pull out the "Treat People Right" card and walk through the two sides of the card (e.g., "Yes, I've learned to treat people right by treating them with dignity by showing respect. I also learned how to show people respect with these five approaches and how to practice empathy using the *Empathy Triad*.")

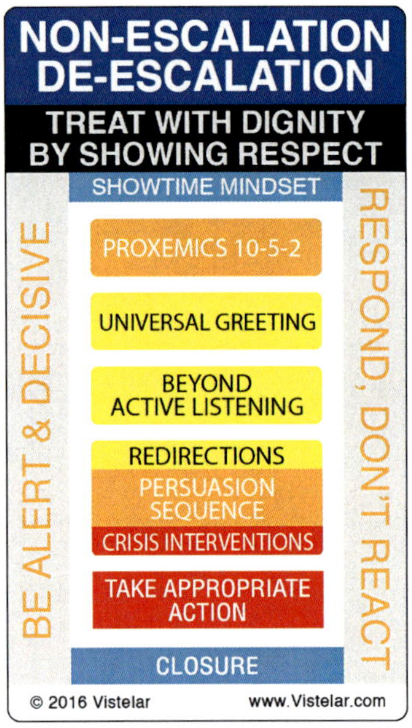

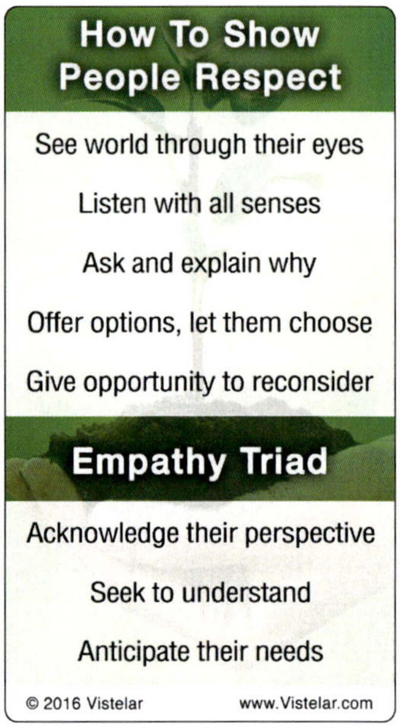

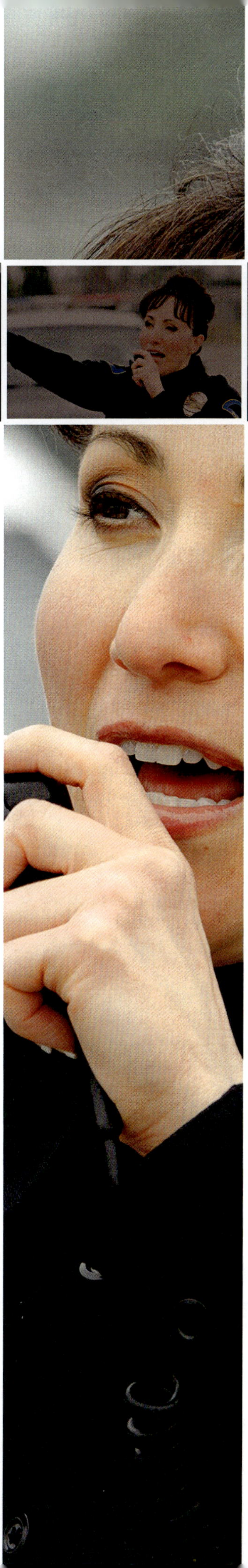

Pulling It All Together

Review: Systemized Structure of Tactics

The emphasis throughout this manual has been on non-escalation, using the tactics of *Showing Respect*, *Practicing Empathy*, *Be Alert & Decisive*; *Respond Don't React*, *Showtime Mindset*, *Proxemics 10-5-2*, *Universal Greeting* and *Beyond Active Listening*.

When possible, it is always better to prevent conflict from starting, rather than having to use the de-escalation tactics of *Redirections*, *Persuasion Sequence* and *Crisis Interventions*.

- *Redirections*: when someone verbally abuses you, bullies you, or is on a rambling tangent from what you are trying to accomplish.
- *Persuasion Sequence*: when someone is questioning, resisting or refusing a request.
- *Crisis Interventions*: when someone is in crisis and displaying at-risk behaviors.

If used consistently, these de-escalation tactics enable you to decrease the intensity of conflict situations, maintain everyone's safety, and shift conflict situations to a positive *Closure*.

However, prior to using a de-escalation tactic, you should always ask yourself if it would be more appropriate to apply the tactic of *Beyond Active Listening* to see if there is any information you missed that could help in your management of the situation. Remember that you are dealing with a human being, so always be careful to preserve the other person's dignity.

At any point during an interaction, you should be ready to *Take Appropriate Action* if there is a clearly articulable safety concern. To do this, you must know your options and have a pre-planned response to situations you will likely face ("when-then thinking").

You should also be prepared to *Take Appropriate Action* if an individual continues to question, resist or refuse a request despite your efforts to give him or her every opportunity to cooperate by using the three-step *Persuasion Sequence*.

Finally, you should try to end every interaction with a positive *Closure* with the two goals of achieving the best possible outcome and establishing a positive foundation for any future interactions.

Beyond the above summary, here is a quick review of the principles and tactics you have learned in this manual.

- Treat people with dignity by showing respect
- Show people respect by:
  - Seeing the world through their eyes
  - Listening with all your senses
  - Asking and explaining why
  - Offering options and letting them choose
  - Giving an opportunity to reconsider
- Practice *Empathy* by applying the *Empathy Triad:*
  - Acknowledge the other person's perspective
  - Seek to understand the other person
  - Anticipate the other person's needs
- Don't speak reactively
- Know your conflict triggers and how to maintain your *Emotional Equilibrium* when faced with them
- Be careful your spoken words, non-verbals and paraverbals (especially your tone of voice) don't set off the *Conflict Triggers* of others
- Remain alert, be decisive and have a preplanned practice response in mind
- Establish a *Showtime Mindset* in advance of any interaction where you anticipate or are faced with conflict
- Be attentive to *Proxemics 10-5-2*
- Use the *Universal Greeting* in all initial interactions
- Actively listen, and when conflict arises, go *Beyond Active Listening*
- De-escalate conflict situations with:
  - *Redirections*

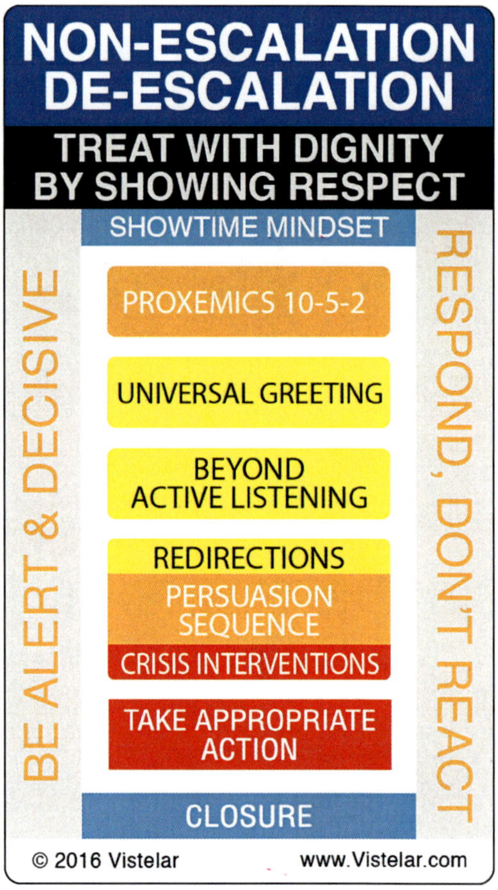

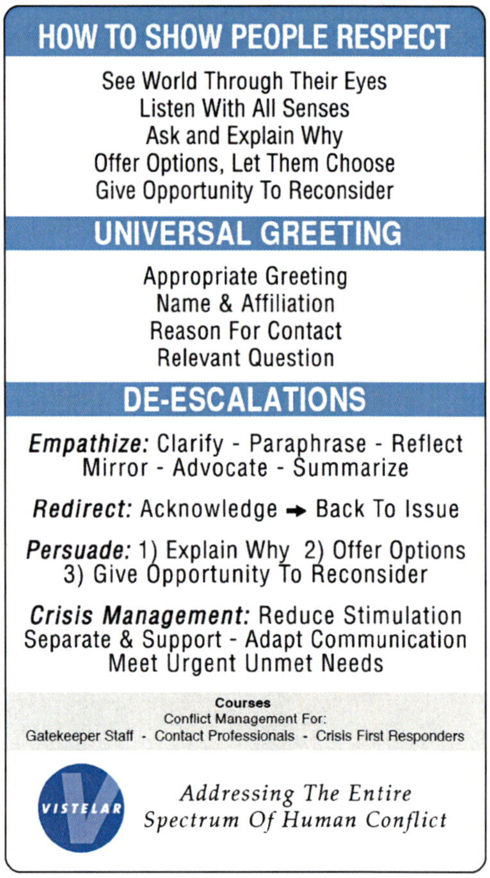

  - *Persuasion Sequence*
  - *Crisis Interventions*
- Plan for when word-based tactics fail, and when necessary, *Take Appropriate Action*
- Effectively close every interaction

Core Principle Revisited

The core principle of customer service and conflict management that serves as the foundation of everything Vistelar teaches is:

Treat people with dignity by showing respect even if you disagree with them.

The primary reason to do this is because acknowledging people's inherent value as human beings, no matter what the circumstances, is the human thing to do.

This quote emphasizes this point. We treat people right because of who we are, not in response to who they are or how they may be behaving.

"We treat people like ladies and gentlemen not necessarily because they are, but because we are."

North Dakota Highway Patrol

Framework: Six Cs Of Conflict Management

Let's return to how the non-escalation, de-escalation and ending-an-interaction tactics apply to Vistelar's *Point-Of-Impact Conflict Management Framework*™.

The blue boxes in the graphic describe the three elements of all interactions.

The primary goals of *Context*, *Contact* and *Closure* are non-escalation, achieving the best possible outcome, and establishing a positive foundation for any future interactions.

The red boxes in the graphic describe what can happen when interactions escalate.

The primary goals in the face of *Conflict*, *Crisis* or *Combat* are de-escalation, everyone's safety, and shifting the situation to a positive outcome.

Note that all interactions have a *Context*, *Contact* and *Closure* elements but only some interactions progress to *Conflict*, *Crisis* and/or *Combat*.

Please think back to the tactics you've learned and consider as to which element of an interaction each tactic would be most likely used.

Inconsistency Is The Enemy Of Peace

In many situations, an individual can interact with multiple campus public safety officers during a single encounter. If each officer treats this individual differently, especially if he or she is displaying bad or criminal behavior, it can be a recipe for disaster.

For example, this can happen where the first responders are managing the situation respectfully and competently but then backup arrives and destroys the positive groundwork that has been laid.

In any environment where several people interact with a single individual, it is critically important that everyone consistently applies effective conflict management principles and tactics. Otherwise, the inconsistency in how a person is treated can actually make things worse.

"Inconsistency is the enemy of peace."

Joel Lashley, author of *Confidence In Conflict For Healthcare Professionals*

If you have one officer using the skills learned in this manual, but then have other officers "speaking reactively" and blurting out what first pops into their mind, the situation will likely escalate. You don't want one officer using the appropriate tactics, another ignoring the situation, someone else killing the individual with kindness, a fourth officer defending their ego to save face and someone else doing things that set off the individual's conflict triggers.

Such inconsistency will almost always empower a badly-behaving individual to escalate his or her actions.

In contrast, if an individual is acting out and everyone interacting with that person consistently applies the appropriate conflict management principles and tactics, the likelihood of a positive *Closure* is much greater.

BE CONSISTENT IN HOW YOU TREAT PEOPLE

INCONSISTENCY IS THE ENEMY OF PEACE

Another Strategy To Reduce Conflict

There is another conflict management strategy that is often ignored, but can have a significant impact on the prevalence of conflict within a campus public safety agency — with students, campus staff, and the general public.

This strategy is to fix operational issues. For example, with parking citations, if you limit payments to one station during normal business hours, you can prevent a great deal of conflict by allowing payment 24/7 at any district station.

Here are some other examples of operational fixes that can prevent conflict:

- Eliminating or automating steps in a process
- Streamlining bureaucratic procedures or decision processes
- Proactively notifying people of a problem rather than waiting to be contacted
- Reducing or simplifying paperwork

If you apply your new powers of *Empathy* to your operations (seeing the world through the general public's and your employees' eyes), you will be amazed at the ideas for friction-reducing fixes you come up with.

Fixing operational issues so students, the general public and campus staff never have to deal with problems that could cause them conflict is, for a campus public safety agency, is one of the best ways to treat people with dignity.

Management Is Still Required

Effective conflict management at the point of impact — with students, at meetings, in one-on-one discussions, in the hallway, at lunch and within project teams — has immediate benefits.

In addition, it also lays the groundwork for longer-term positive outcomes, such as increased customer satisfaction, reducing citizen complaints, collaboration instead of compromise, people not avoiding conflict or accommodating it by giving in and improved team performance.

However, well-managed conflict is just part of the equation for long-term success. For example:

- If students, faculty & staff and agency employees are treated with dignity, they will feel more emotionally safe and be more willing to share their concerns and problems, but someone still needs to address the concerns and fix the problems.
- Arguments among individuals on campus will be productive instead of destructive, but people still need to know how to collaborate and negotiate true win-win agreements.
- Conflict will get resolved rather than being allowed to fester, but management still needs to give clear direction, hold people accountable and evaluate performance.

Poorly-managed conflict at the point of impact is a huge roadblock to organizational performance, and addressing this issue can have a significant impact. However, it is not a cure-all — you still need strong management for all the benefits of effective conflict management to be realized.

SOCIAL CONTRACT

VOLUNTARY AGREEMENT BY ALL EMPLOYEES TO CONSISTENTLY TREAT EVERYONE WITH DIGNITY BY SHOWING RESPECT

And, relative to management, please remember *The Ultimate Goal* of the training provided by this manual — to develop a professional *Social Contract*: a voluntary agreement by all employees to consistently treat everyone with dignity by showing respect.

If you are a boss, start the "expectation contracting" process right way: make it crystal clear how you expect students, campus staff and employees to be treated, set a good example and encourage members of your team to set an example — "I'm going to treat you with dignity by showing you respect. I ask the same from you".

A More Efficient Approach

We sometimes hear that, while Vistelar's conflict management tactics are extremely effective, they may not always seem the most efficient.

With students and faculty & staff, it might seem more efficient to just tell them what to do, to not listen to them, and when asked why, to just say "because I told you so." And, with employees, it might seem more efficient to cut off debate, make a quick decision or ask people to hold their tongues.

However, that is false efficiency. The data[9] is crystal clear that using principles and tactics that show people respect just work better, so on the whole, they are far more efficient.

Sure, with students and faculty & staff it takes time to really listen and not interrupt, to give explanations for your requests and to offer options from which to choose. And, with employees it takes time to not end a meeting until everyone has talked, to encourage people who are upset to express their frustrations, and to allow honest discussion without fear of retribution.

All this takes time, but in the short and long term, showing people respect is both more effective AND more efficient in managing conflict, delivering exceptional customer service and driving increased team performance.

Conflict Must Be Addressed Head-On

From the 1980s through the mid-2000s, Vistelar's trainers worked primarily with law enforcement who generally aren't shy about addressing conflict head-on.

Then, in the mid-2000s, we started working in other markets, such as healthcare, education and business where we found that many people struggled with conflict. As a result, they would avoid it at all costs or accommodate people by giving in just to appease them.

Conflict avoidance and accommodation can cause such problems as:

- Conflicts never getting resolved
- Resentment and lowered self-esteem
- Reinforcement of inappropriate behavior

- Conflicts actually escalating to emotional or physical violence

Vistelar's primary focus continues to be in working with "contact professionals," like police officers, who are comfortable with conflict but want to learn how to be more effective at managing it.

However, we find ourselves spending more and more time working with individuals and teams to provide them with the *knowledge*, *skills* and *abilities* to effectively manage conflict so they don't end up avoiding it or accommodating people by giving in. We want our students to be able to deal with conflict head-on, rather than shying away from it.

> *"In surveys of European and American executives, fully 85% of them acknowledge they have issues or concerns at work that they were afraid to raise. Afraid of the conflict that would provoke, afraid to get embroiled in arguments they did not know how to manage and they were bound to lose."*
>
> Margaret Heffernan, TED Talk: Dare To Disagree (1955 - present)

Just The Beginning

In managing conflict, there is a huge difference between knowledge, skills and abilities.

Knowledge — understanding a body of information related to the performance of a function

Skill — an observable competence to perform a learned psychomotor act

Ability — competence to perform an observable behavior in a real-world situation

DEVELOP THE ABILITY TO PERFORM YOUR CONFLICT MANAGEMENT SKILLS IN REAL-WORLD SITUATIONS

PRACTICE. PRACTICE. PRACTICE.

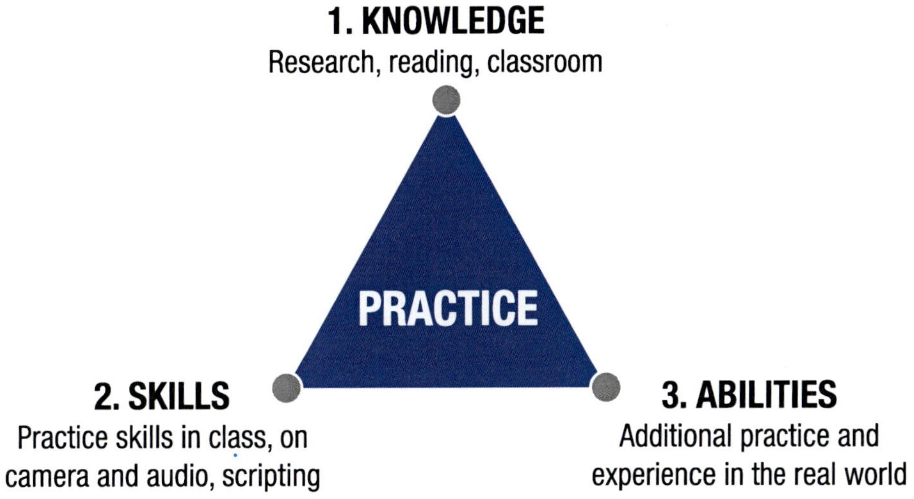

By reading and studying this manual, you can obtain the *knowledge* of how to be effective at conflict management. Vistelar's books, online courses and live workshops are other avenues for obtaining this knowledge.

However, when someone is dealing with conflict, just having *knowledge* is not nearly enough. You also need conflict-management *skills* including written scripts, and most importantly, the ability to perform those skills in real-world situations.

"Knowing is not enough; we must apply. Willing is not enough; we must do."

Johann Wolfgang von Goethe, German writer (1749 - 1832)

Therefore, please view this manual and other training you may receive from Vistelar as just the beginning. Please realize that, in real-world situations, managing conflict will rarely go as planned. Therefore, you must develop your conflict management *knowledge*, *skills* and *abilities* to a level where you can adapt to the situation and effectively handle whatever comes at you.

"Many skills – in particular, tactical communication skills – are perishable and need to be reinforced and practiced on a regular basis."

PERF: *Integrating Communications, Assessment, and Tactics Training Guide For Diffusing Critical Incidents* — October 2016

To move beyond from just having *knowledge* to having skills, you could attend an instructor-led online or in-person program where we provide the opportunity to demonstrate observable competence in the skills we teach.

Then, to develop your conflict management *abilities*, you could attend one of our longer classes where we have time for practice in simulations of real-world situations.

However, to become truly effective at conflict management, you must commit to further developing your *skills* and *abilities* by developing your own scripts for the situations you face, putting those scripts to memory, practicing those scripts using all three elements of communication (words, tone of voice, non-verbals) with friends, family members and colleagues, and using the principles and tactics you have learned in this manual in real-world situations.

"Training without practice is a fool's bet."

Dave Young, Arma Director of Training

When faced with real-world conflict, just winging it does not work. Instead, you need lots of "arrows" in your quiver that you have memorized and are comfortable and competent in using because you have baked them into your mental muscle memory via extensive practice and use.

Remember that effective conflict management is a performance so, before you go on stage, you must practice your lines, body language, facial expressions and stage positioning, as well as practice meshing the verbal elements of an interaction with the physical. Then, you need lots of stage time.

"Amateurs practice until they get it right. Professionals practice until they can't get it wrong."

Anonymous

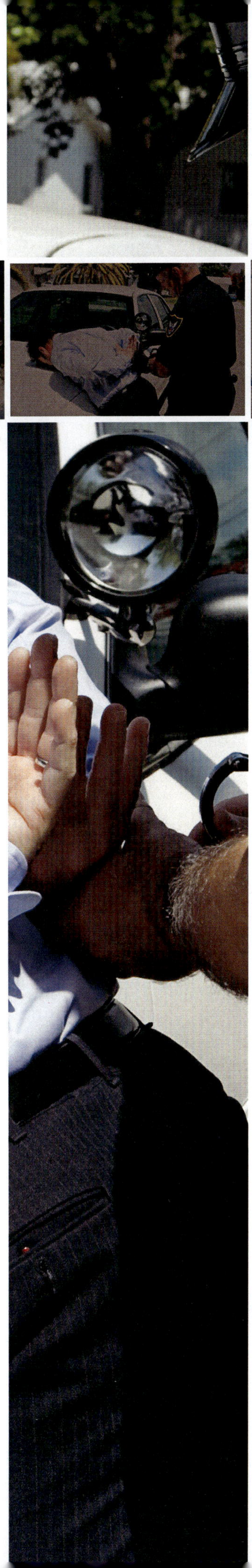

Additional Information

Fire Drills

All of Vistelar's in-person training programs use a "fire drill vs. fire talk" approach.

Class time emphasizes student interaction, scenario-based skill practice (using a proprietary video recording/review technology), analysis of real-life events captured on video, and memorable real-life stories ("peace stories") that illustrate the positive outcomes resulting from use of Vistelar's methodologies.

The goal of this approach is for our students to develop the knowledge, skills and abilities to manage real situations in the real world. However, there is never enough time in class to develop true proficiency.

Therefore, it is essential you practice the tactics listed below on an ongoing basis by developing "fire drills" optimized for your style of learning.

- *Conflict Triggers*
- *Treat With Dignity By Showing Respect*
- *Be Alert & Responsive; Respond, Don't React*
- *Showtime Mindset*
- *Proxemics 10-5-2*
- *Universal Greeting*
- *Beyond Active Listening*
- *Redirections*
- *Persuasion Sequence*
- *Crisis Interventions*
- *Take Appropriate Action*
- *Closure*

Other Resources

Vistelar offers our training via speaking engagements, workshops, and instructor schools using both live and online methods of instruction.

To download a description of Vistelar's campus public safety training programs, go to:

vistelar.com/course-descriptions

If you are a certified Vistelar instructor, you can access our Member Website by going to:

vistelaronline.com

Beyond the above, we obviously have much more to share about conflict management via our books, manuals, online programs, workshops, instructor schools and consulting services.

If you would like to learn more about what Vistelar offers, please access any or all of the additional resources listed below. We look forward to helping you further in better managing conflict in both your work and personal lives.

Live Training

Access our training calendar with registration information for upcoming in-person conflict management training programs —

www.vistelar.com/training-calendar

Get information about contracting with Vistelar to provide a customized conflict management training program for your agency, company, organization or group — www.vistelar.com/custom-onsite

Get information about hosting a Vistelar training program at your facility and receiving free slots in the hosted class — www.vistelar.com/host-a-class

Publications

Access our listing of online conflict management training programs, delivered using both virtual instructor-led and on-demand training methods — www.vistelar.com/online-courses

Access our online shopping cart with Vistelar books, manuals, online courses, workbooks, apparel and other products — www.vistelar.com/shopping-cart

Download a PDF of one or more of Vistelar's 16-page market-specific training program descriptions — www.vistelar.com/course-descriptions

Consulting

Get information about booking a Vistelar speaker to educate your

audience on such topics as conflict management, crisis intervention, personal safety awareness & protection, bystander mobilization, and workplace violence (including active shooter) — www.vistelar.com/speaking

Get information about Vistelar's workplace security/safety consulting services (review/analysis of and recommendations for: policies & procedures, environmental & procedural vulnerability, physical security technology, security personnel staffing, conflict management training) —

www.vistelar.com/consulting

About Vistelar

This manual was developed by Vistelar, a consulting and training institute focused on addressing the entire spectrum of human conflict at the point of impact — from before an interaction begins through to the consequences of how an interaction is managed.

Vistelar offers a wide range of training programs that address how to:

- Provide better customer service
- Predict, prevent and mitigate conflict
- Avert verbal and physical attacks
- De-escalate resistance, anger and abuse
- Control crisis and aggression
- Effectively manage physical violence

The results at the organizational level are:

- Higher levels of customer satisfaction
- Improved team performance, morale and safety
- Reduced complaints, liabilities and injuries
- Protected reputation, culture and business continuity
- Reduced harm from emotional and physical violence
- Decreased stress levels, lateral violence and bullying
- Less compassion fatigue, absenteeism and turnover
- Not having a damaging video show up on YouTube or the evening news

Our training is focused on the point of impact — the short period of time when disagreements, insults or gateway behaviors, such as swearing or aggressive posturing, can escalate to conflict and on to emotional and/or physical violence. We train "contact professionals" who directly interact with the general public or an organization's clients, and organizational teams who want to improve their performance by better managing conflict.

Vistelar's methodologies have been proven in real-world environments for over thirty years and are the subject of several books and training manuals in Vistelar's Confidence In Conflict and Conflict Management series[10].

TRAINING PROGRAMS

ENTIRE SPECTRUM OF HUMAN CONFLICT

NON-ESCALATION DE-ESCALATION

Conflict Management For:
- Gatekeeper Staff
- Contact Professionals
- Crisis First Responders

PHYSICAL ALTERNATIVES

- Principles of Subject Control 1 & 2
- Non-Lethal Weapons
- Lethal Weapons

Over 50 Specialty Courses

Tactics taught, relative emphasis on each tactic, and level of intrusiveness depend on student's rules of engagement, environments, applications and roles within their organization

Speaking - Workshops - Instructor Schools
Live - Online - Blended

VISTELAR

Addressing The Entire Spectrum Of Human Conflict

POINT-OF-IMPACT CONFLICT MANAGEMENT TRAINING

LEARN HOW TO:
- Provide better customer service
- Predict, prevent and mitigate conflict
- Avert verbal and physical attacks
- De-escalate conflict
- Control crisis and aggression
- Handle physical violence

BENEFITS:
- Higher levels of customer satisfaction
- Reduced complaints, liabilities & injuries
- Improved team performance and morale
- Protected reputation, culture, business continuity and employee safety
- Reduced workplace violence
- Not having a damaging video show up on YouTube or the evening news

WHO WE TRAIN:
- Contact professionals who directly interact with the general public or an organization's clients
- Organizational teams who want to improve their performance by better managing conflict.

We offer our training via speaking engagements, workshops, and instructor schools — using both live and online methods of instruction.

Our vision is to make the world safer by teaching everyone how to treat each other with dignity by showing respect.

Origins of Vistelar

The origins of Vistelar date back to the early 1980s when Gary T. Klugiewicz, a nationally known defensive tactics trainer and future co-founder of Vistelar, helped originate Wisconsin's "unified tactical training" systems (DAAT, P.O.S.C.®).

Gary T. Klugiewicz

Since the mid-80s, every police officer, jail/juvenile detention officer and prison probation/parole officer is trained in these systems. In the mid-90s, he helped developed Professional Communications Skills (PCS), the communications component of Wisconsin's training system.

Over the last three decades, Gary has implemented this unified tactical training system in scores of law enforcement agencies, correctional institutions and healthcare/mental health organizations throughout the United States. He also has been a national instructor for Calibre Press's Street Survival Seminar®, Team One Network, Redman Protective Gear and PoliceOne. Gary retired from the Milwaukee County Sheriff 's Department in 2001 after 25 years in service.

Dave Young

In 1992, Gary started working closely with Dave Young, a nationally recognized defensive tactics trainer of law enforcement, corrections and the military. Gary and Dave worked together for over 17 years before founding Vistelar in 2009.

Allen Oelschlaeger

During this time, Gary and Dave worked with PoliceOne, ILEETA, and Force Science Research, and collaborated with many subject matter experts in the field of law enforcement and healthcare training, such as Robert Lindsey, Daniel Vega, Dr. Kevin Parsons, Charles Remsberg, Bob Willis, Dr. George Thompson, Col. Dave Grossman, Jack Hoban, Joel Lashley, and Jeff Mehring.

Vistelar was founded to enable Gary and Dave to disseminate their comprehensive training programs — that *address the entire spectrum of human conflict* — to a wider range of markets, including college public safety, healthcare, loss prevention, security, education, hospitality, business, transit and corrections.

Since the founding of Vistelar by Gary, Dave and business executive, Allen Oelschlaeger, the company has extended its reach, published several books and manuals in its *Confidence In Conflict* series, introduced several conflict management online training programs, and greatly expanded its team of employees, trainers, advisors and certified instructors.

Today Vistelar is a world leader in point-of-impact conflict management training, which it offers as a comprehensive system of non-escalation and de-escalation coupled with physical alternatives.

To learn more:

Call: 877-690-8230
Email: info@vistelar.com
Visit: www.vistelar.com

Acknowledgments

The authors would like to thank the many people who contributed to the subject matter of this manual over the span of the last 30+ years.

- Mike Delvaux — retired Captain, Wisconsin Department of Corrections
- Katie Dill — Vistelar Trainer
- Harry Dolan — retired Chief, Raleigh Police Department
- Jane Dresser — Director, Medical-Psychiatric Nursing Consultants, Inc.
- Andrew Garrison — President, BodyFacts Wellness Services
- Peter Harrell, Jr. — President, Harrell Communications
- Jack Hoban — President, Resolution Group International
- Peter Jaskulski — retired Captain, Milwaukee County Sheriff's Department
- Joel Lashley — Security Supervisor, Aurora Healthcare
- Chan Lee — Owner, J.K. Lee Black Belt Academy
- Robert Lindsey — retired Colonel, Jefferson Parish Sheriff's Office
- Gary Loop — President, Loop Group, LLC
- Jeff Mehring — retired Regional Director of Safety and Security, Wheaton-Franciscan Healthcare
- Dennis Nourse — Director, Mediation Center of Waukesha County
- Tony Pinelle — retired Chief, Public Safety Colorado Mental Health
- Joe Potterton — Security Operations Manager, The Children's Hospital of Philadelphia
- Vince Rampulla — VP Loss Prevention and Security, Roundy's Supermarkets, Inc.
- Charles Remsberg and Dennis Anderson — Founders, Calibre Press
- Dick Sem — President, Sem Security Management
- William Singleton — Partner, Vistelar
- Anthony Sherman — President, Genesis Group RMS
- Karen Stentz Huebner, PhD. — President, Purposeful Development Associates
- George Thompson, PhD. — Founder, Verbal Judo Institute
- Kati Tillema — Partner, Vistelar
- Pablo Velazquez — Vistelar Trainer
- Daniel Vega, M.S.W. — Crisis Intervention Specialist, Tacoma, WA
- Derick Washington, Sr. — retired Lieutenant, Milwaukee County Sheriff's Office
- Jill Weisensel — Lieutenant, Marquette University Police Department
- Robert Whiteside — Executive Director, Security Mission Health
- Robert Willis — formerly Street Survival Instructor, Northeast Wisconsin Technical College
- Debbie Zwicky — Vistelar Trainer

Endnotes

[1] Alper, S., Tjosvold, D., & Law, K.S. (2000). Conflict Management, Efficacy, and Performance in Organizational Teams. *Personnel Psychology*. Vol 53, Issue 3, pp. 625-642

[2] DeChurch, L.A. & Marks, M.A. (2001). Maximizing the Benefits of Task Conflict: The Role of Conflict Management. *The International Journal of Conflict Management*. Vol. 12, No. 1, pp. 4-22

Amason, A.C. (1996). Distinguishing the effects of functional and dysfunctional conflict on strategic decision making: Resolving a paradox for top management teams. *Academy of Management Journal*, 39, pp.123–148

[3] "A small percentage of officers account for a disproportionate percentage of total citizen complaints. Excessive force and discourtesy were often the most common allegations lodged, and younger officers and those with less experience generally received a greater number of complaints. Providing those officers with appropriate training in empathy, professionalism, and de-escalation can help reduce those complaints."

Terell, W. & Ingram, J.R. (2016). Citizen Complaints Against the Police: An Eight City Examination. *Police Quarterly*. Vol. 19(2) pp. 150–179

[4] Research shows that, when it comes to customer service and organizational trust, people generally choose the organization with the better reputation. Additionally, those surveys show people have the least satisfaction with companies that fail to acknowledge the bad thing that happened and fail to try and make it right. Conflict management training equip people to do all of the above: build and protect the organizational reputation and culture, acknowledge missteps, and verbally de-escalate and repair them.

Bettenhausen K.L. (1991). Five years of groups research: What we have learned and what needs to be addressed. *Journal of Management*, 17, pp. 345–381

Bettenhausen K.L & Murnighan J.K. (1991). The development of an intragroup norm and the effects of interpersonal and structural challenges. *Administrative Science Quarterly*, 36, pp. 20–35

[5] Alper, S., Tjosvold, D., & Law, K.S. (2000). Conflict Management, Efficacy, and Performance in Organizational Teams. *Personnel Psychology*. Vol. 53, Issue 3, pp. 625–642

[6] Alper, S., Tjosvold, D., & Law, K.S. (2000). Conflict Management, Efficacy, and Performance in Organizational Teams. *Personnel Psychology*. Vol. 53, Issue 3, pp. 625–642

[7] Greenwald, A.G. and Krieger L.H. (2006) *Implicit Bias: Scientific Foundations*, 94 Cal. L. Rev. 945

[8] Yudkin, Daniel & Rothmund, Tobias & Twardawski, Mathias & Thalla, Natasha & J Van Bavel, Jay. (2016). Reflexive Intergroup Bias in Third-Party Punishment. *Journal of Experimental Psychology* General. pp. 145

[9] Huntington, B., & Kuhn, N. (2003). Communication gaffes: A root cause of malpractice claims. *Baylor University Medical Centre Proceedings*, 16(2), pp.157-161

Matsumoto, D., Frank, M.G., & Hwang, H. S. *Nonverbal Communication: Science and Applications.* Los Angeles: Sage Publications Inc., 2012.

[10] Matsumoto, D., Frank, M.G., & Hwang, H. S. *Nonverbal Communication: Science and Applications.* Sage Publications Inc., 2012.

Maccario, C. J. (2012). Aviation Security and Nonverbal Behavior. In *Nonverbal Communication: Science and Applications* (pp. 147-154)

Bibliography

De Becker, Gavin. *The Gift of Fear and Other Survival Signals that Protect Us From Violence.* Dell, 1999.

Elgin, Suzette Haden. *The Gentle Art of Verbal Self-Defense at Work.* Prentice Hall, 2000.

Fehr, B. J., & Exline, R. V. Social visual interactions: A conceptual and literature review. A.W. Siegman & S. Feldstein (Editors), *Nonverbal Behavior and Communication*, Psychology Press, 1987, pp. 225-326

Frank, M. G. & Eckman, P. (1997). The ability to detect deceit generalizes across different types of high-stake lies. *Journal of Personality and Social Psychology*, 72, 1429-1439

Hall, E. T. (1963). A system for the notation of proxemic behaviors. *American Anthropologist*, 65, 1003-1026

Hoban, Jack E. *The Ethical Warrior: Values, Morals and Ethics - For Life, Work and Service.* CreateSpace, 2012.

Huntington, B., & Kuhn, N. (2003). Communication gaffes: A root cause of malpractice claims. *Baylor University Medical Centre Proceedings*, 16(2), 157-161

Knapp, M. L., & Hall, J. A. *Nonverbal Communication in Human Interaction.* Wadsworth Publishing, 2013.

Gilmartin, Kevin, M. *Emotional survival for law enforcement: A guide for officers and their families.* E-S Press, 2002.

Grossman, Dave. *On Killing: The Psychological Cost of Learning to Kill in War and Society.* Back Bay Books, 2009.

Horn, Sam. *Tongue Fu!: How to Deflect, Disarm, and Defuse Any Verbal Conflict.* St. Martin's Griffin, 1997.

Katz, Neil H. et. al. *Communication & Conflict Resolution Skills.* Kendall Hunt Publishing, 1992.

Klugiewicz, Gary et. al. *Conflict Management For Law Enforcement.* Truths Publishing, 2016.

Lashley, Joel. *Confidence In Conflict For Healthcare Professionals: Creating an Environment of Care that is Incompatible with Violence.* Truths Publishing, 2015.

Jaskulski, Pete. *Confidence in Conflict for Sports Officials: Practical Tips for Staying Out of the Cross Fire and Keeping Peace During the Game.* Truths Publishing, 2015.

Mangold, Kathy. *Confidence In Conflict For Everyday Life: How to Prevent and Manage the Inevitable Conflict in Your Work and Personal Life.* Truths Publishing, 2014.

Matsumoto, D., Frank, M.G., & Hwang, H. S. *Nonverbal Communication: Science and Applications.* Sage Publications Inc., 2012.

Remsberg, Charles et. al. *Street Survival: Tactics For Armed Encounters.* Calibre Press, 1987.

Weisensel, Jill. *Confidence In Conflict For Campus Life: The Must-Have Safety Resource for Every College and College-Bound Student.* Truths Publishing, 2014.

Young, Dave. *How to Defend Your Family and Home: Outsmart an Invader, Secure Your Home, Prevent a Burglary and Protect Your Loved Ones from Any Threat.* Page Street Publishing, 2017.